QUANTUM
TECHNOLOGY

www.royalcollins.com

QUANTUM TECHNOLOGY

The Power to Disrupt the Future

KEVIN CHEN

Books Beyond Boundaries

ROYAL COLLINS

Quantum Technology: The Power to Disrupt the Future

Kevin Chen

First published in 2024 by Royal Collins Publishing Group Inc.
Groupe Publication Royal Collins Inc.
BKM Royalcollins Publishers Private Limited

Headquarters: 550-555 boul. René-Lévesque O Montréal (Québec) H2Z1B1 Canada
India office: 805 Hemkunt House, 8th Floor, Rajendra Place, New Delhi 110 008

10 9 8 7 6 5 4 3 2 1

ISBN: 978-1-4878-1177-8

To find out more about our publications, please visit www.royalcollins.com.

CONTENTS

Future Section
Toward the Quantum Era

Basic Section

DISCOVERING QUANTUM MECHANICS

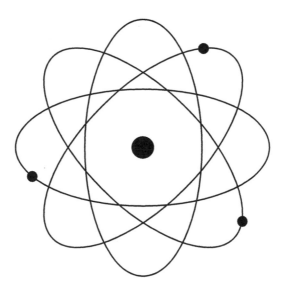

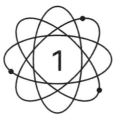

THE QUANTUM ERA

1.1 Introduction

If we were to select the greatest epochs in the history of physics, they would undoubtedly be the late 17th and early 20th centuries.

At the end of the 17th century, marked by the publication of Newton's *Mathematical Principles of Natural Philosophy*, humankind entered the era of classical physics. At the beginning of the 20th century, physicists began to explore the silent and invisible world of atoms, nuclei, and elementary particles, and following theoretical and experimental discussions, a new kingdom was born, namely the quantum kingdom.

Compared with classical physics, the quantum era, nearly three hundred years later, was full of mystery and brilliance. The birth of the theory of relativity and quantum theory not only created a whole new kingdom of the physical world but also completely overthrew and reconstructed the entire system of physics, which has far-reaching effects today.

1.1.1 The Classical Mechanics Age

Today, few people are unaware of Newton's greatness, who brought humankind into the age of classical physics in 1688 with the publication of his work

Mathematical Principles of Natural Philosophy. Newton's major accomplishments are gathered here: the study of universal gravitation and the three laws of mechanics.

Newton believed that Earth exerts a force on objects on its surface and that this force is in accordance with the law of universal gravitation and proved and perfected Kepler's law on the motion of celestial bodies. The process of Newton's discovery of gravity is not new to many people, as we are all familiar with the story of Newton and the apple, an unlucky young man to discover the law of universal gravitation by becoming interested in the apple that hit him.

Universal gravitation is easy to understand. All objects are attracted to each other, but this seemingly simple explanation is a great discovery. Universal gravitation will allow people to study motion, from the movement of Earth to celestial bodies.

However, Newton's law of universal gravitation is not the first attempt by man to explain the mysterious motion of the universe. In fact, before Newton, many scientists were already interested in the motion of celestial bodies. They made fruitful research results, the most famous of which is Kepler's laws, which were applied to Newton's discovery of the law of universal gravitation. However, compared to the previous research results, Newton's theory is more systematic, comprehensive, and capable of explaining many natural phenomena. The expression of this law is also simpler—any two mass points attract each other, and the direction of gravity is on the line connecting the mass points. The magnitude of this gravity is proportional to the product of the masses of the mass points and inversely proportional to the square of the distance. It is with Newton's law of universal gravitation that the mysteries of the universe can be solved. We can use it to reveal and study the laws of planetary motion around stars and the laws of satellite orbit around planets.

In addition, Newton explained his three laws of mechanics, the law of inertia, the law of acceleration, and the law of action and reaction.

Before Newton, it was taken for granted that the motion of an object requires force propulsion. If the object is to move continuously, it must be continuously given force propulsion, just like pushing a car without power. Once the force is not applied, it will stop. This is like Aristotle's view that light objects fall slower than heavier objects.

Newton believed that when the object is not subject to the action of external forces, it will remain at rest or in a uniform, straight motion. Only when the object's state of motion changes, for example, from rest to motion, from uniform motion to accelerated motion, and from straight motion to curvilinear motion, it needs the role of force to change the object's direction of motion. In more concise words, "All objects will remain in a state of rest or uniform motion in a straight line unless compelled to change that state by external forces." In other words, rest or uniform straight motion is the object's most "natural" state; if it is not subject to external forces, it will remain in this state forever. This fundamentally changes the old idea that people take the need to force the object to move for granted, and this is Newton's law of inertia.

Acceleration is a change in the speed of an object in motion, which can either increase or decrease, and we can consider the latter as a negative acceleration. The cause of the acceleration of the object is, of course, force. In other words, force is required to transition an object from motion to rest, from rest to motion, or to increase or decrease the velocity of a moving object.

Newton attributed all physical motion and deformation to the presence of "force." Without force, everything should not change its state of motion; if there is force, the object will move or deform, and the greater the force, the more obvious the motion.

Since Newton created classical mechanics, humankind used classical mechanics to carry out the First Industrial Revolution, which greatly increased productivity. Later the Second Industrial Revolution also has the shadow of classical mechanics. Until today, Newton's classical mechanics is still guiding all aspects of human life, from the Mars rover landing on Mars to the bullet penetrating the target, all of which can need to use classical mechanics. It can be said that Newton deeply influenced the human world after the 17th century and accelerated the process of technological revolution to a certain extent.

1.1.2 Challenges to Classical Physics

Although classical physics appears complete, this glorious era soon encountered new challenges. With the advancement of science and the transformation of the world, Newton's mechanics unexpectedly experienced "malfunctions" in certain special application scenarios. One of the typical problems mentioned by Kelvin in his lecture titled "Nineteenth-Century Cloud Sover the Dynamical Theory of Heat and Light" was the issue of black body radiation.

A black body is an ideal model established by physicists in the realm of thermodynamics. It is a standard object for studying thermal radiation laws independent of the specific material properties. The black body absorbs all incoming electromagnetic radiation without reflecting or transmitting it. In other words, the absorption coefficient of the black body for any wavelength of an electromagnetic wave is 1, and the transmission coefficient is 0. Any object with a temperature higher than absolute zero can emit thermal radiation, and the higher the temperature, the greater the total energy emitted, including a greater proportion of short-wave components. As the temperature increases, the electromagnetic waves emitted by a black body are called black body radiation.

By measuring the radiation emitted by black bodies, physicists discovered that black body radiation did not behave as predicted by classical theories, suggesting it would tend toward infinity in the ultraviolet region. Instead, it peaked in the visible light region of the spectrum, as shown in figure 1. In other words, as the temperature rises, the energy of radiation initially reaches a peak and then decreases as the wavelength decreases. The physics theories at that time were unable to explain this phenomenon, leaving physicists puzzled and unable to comprehend this strange, non-theoretical data.

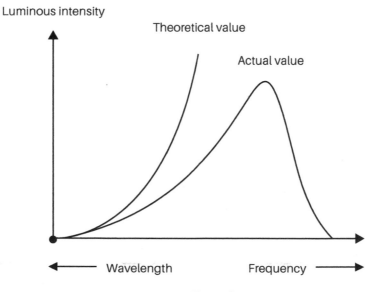

Figure 1

Furthermore, in 1898, the Curie couple discovered the elements polonium and radium, revealing that atoms are no longer the smallest units composing matter but rather have complex structures. In 1911, British physicist Rutherford proposed the famous atomic model based on his experiments on the scattering of alpha particles, stating that an atom's positive charge and mass are concentrated in a small central nucleus while electrons orbit around the nucleus.

However, this model raised a question: why aren't the negatively charged electrons in the outer shell of an atom attracted to the positively charged atomic nucleus and pulled into the nucleus? According to classical electrodynamics, the electrons orbiting the atomic nucleus would continuously radiate energy and eventually "collapse" into the nucleus. Yet, atoms do exist stably in the real world. This is also an unexplainable phenomenon within classical physics.

What classical physics cannot explain includes the photoelectric effect. The photoelectric effect is the phenomenon where electrons are emitted when a beam of light strikes a metal surface. This phenomenon is quite peculiar. Normally, electrons are firmly bound to the atoms on the metal surface, but these electrons become active once illuminated by a certain light. However, it is perplexing that whether light can eject electrons from the same metal surface does not depend on the intensity of the light but rather on its frequency. The wave theory of classical physics does not apply to this phenomenon.

Furthermore, the existence of atomic spectra, specific heat in solids, and the stability of atoms, among other issues, increasingly highlight the limitations of classical physics. People gradually realized the inadequacy of classical mechanics and discovered its flaws. In Newton's classical mechanics, time and space are absolute, high-speed and low-speed motion is absolute, and the microcosm and macrocosm are also absolute entities. In this context, quantum mechanics, based on the microscopic world, began to brew and emerge.

In 1900, addressing the problem of black body radiation, German scientist Max Planck put forward a bold assumption: when an object emits or absorbs radiation, the change in energy occurs discontinuously in discrete quantities, which are multiples of a certain value. Subsequently, Planck formulated the famous "Planck's Law" and provided the energy distribution of black body radiation. On December 14 of the same year, Planck presented his article "On the Law of Energy Distribution in Normal Spectra" to the German Physical

Society, reporting his bold hypothesis and introducing the preliminary concept of quantum mechanics, which opened the door to quantum mechanics for humanity.

1.1.3 The Essence of Quantum

Although Planck led humanity into the quantum world, the question remains: what is quantum, exactly? Before understanding quantum, let us first familiarize ourselves with the material world. In fact, throughout history, people have been exploring the composition of matter. The book *Zhuangzi* contains the following sentence: "Take a foot-long stick and keep halving it; no matter how many times you do this, it will never be exhausted." This means that matter can be infinitely divided without ever reaching an end.

So, what is the fundamental unit that constitutes this world? Through the relentless exploration of generation after generation of scientists, they have finally discovered the smallest observable entities of matter—elementary particles. In modern physics, the Standard Model theory indicates 62 types of elementary particles in the world. They form the foundation of the universe, and everything is composed of these 62 particles.

Currently, the process of discovery has been winding and tortuous. In the early 20th century, breakthroughs in physics ushered in the atomic age, and scientists discovered that atoms contain a nucleus with electrons orbiting around them. Atoms themselves are extremely tiny, and the atomic nucleus is even smaller. For example, the radius of a hydrogen atom is approximately 5.3×10^{-11} m or 0.053 nm, while the radius of a hydrogen nucleus is approximately 8.8×10^{-16} m or 0.88 fm. The radius of a hydrogen atom is roughly 60,000 times larger than its nucleus. If we imagine a hydrogen atom to be the size of Earth, with a radius of 6,400 km, then the hydrogen nucleus would be only about 107 m, roughly equivalent to the height of a 35-story building. However, with the advancement of science, it was discovered that these minuscule atomic nuclei could be further divided into even smaller substances.

The substances that make up atomic nuclei can be classified into many types. Initially, scientists identified four: photons, electrons, protons, and neutrons. Later, they gradually discovered other particles, such as positrons, neutrinos, mesons, hyperons, and more. All these particles can be called elementary particles. From a macroscopic perspective, elementary particles are incredibly tiny. Protons and neutrons are relatively larger, with diameters of about 1/100,000,000 cm. As for the other elementary particles, they are even smaller. For example, a neutrino is only 1/10,000 the size of an electron, and an electron is approximately 1/2,000 the size of a proton.

Although these elementary particles are small, they all possess mass. Interestingly, the photon is special—it has zero rest mass. In a 40 W light bulb, billions of photons are emitted every second. On the other hand, the heaviest elementary particle is the hyperon, which is about 340 times more massive than a proton. However, its existence is extremely short-lived, lasting only about 1/10,000,000,000 seconds.

These elementary particles exhibit some fascinating phenomena. For example, under certain circumstances, they can transform into one another. Take the positron and electron as an example—they have the same appearance, weight, and electric charge, but one carries a positive charge while the other carries a negative charge. When they collide, they transform into photons. Similarly, a proton and an antiproton meeting can transform into an antineutron.

Modern physics indicates that these intriguing phenomena of elementary particles arise from "symmetry." If a certain particle exists, there must also exist its antiparticle. When a particle and its antiparticle meet, they annihilate each other, producing photons carrying energy, which is the conversion of matter into energy. Conversely, high-energy particles colliding can also produce new particle-antiparticle pairs, converting energy into matter. This implies that matter and energy can mutually convert.

Not only that but with the development of scientific technology, it has been discovered that elementary particles are composed of even smaller and more fundamental "sub-particles." For example, within protons, there are smaller substances known as quarks. Each proton and neutron is composed of three quarks, while antiparticles are composed of anti-quarks. Even the most advanced electron microscopes cannot directly observe quarks; scientists can only confirm their existence through experiments.

Currently, six quarks are known: up quark, down quark, charm quark, strange quark, top quark, and bottom quark. Quarks are the smallest particles deduced by modern physics. Whether quarks can be further divided or if there are more fundamental substances within quarks remains unknown. If matter can be infinitely divided, then the concept of elementary particles would cease to exist, as any matter could be infinitely divided into smaller parts.

Quantum exists in this microscopic world. During the era of old quantum mechanics, the first decade after Planck introduced the concept of quantum, quantum was often referred to as a physical quantity. At that time, we could understand quantum as indivisible, discontinuous basic units. This is also the Latin meaning of "quantum," representing the amount of matter.

It is essential to note that quantum here does not refer to a specific particle-like atoms, electrons, or protons mentioned earlier. Instead, quantum is merely a conceptual term. Only when combined with specific nouns in certain contexts it represents examples. For example, a light quantum is a photon representing light's fundamental energy unit.

We can imagine climbing a mountain. Continuity is like walking up a gentle slope, where each step can be of any size—half a meter or one meter. In contrast, discontinuity is like going upstairs, where each step can only be an integer multiple of the stair's height. We can go up one or two steps, but we cannot go up half a step. Each step here represents an indivisible basic unit.

Since Planck's time, many physics masters have continuously improved quantum theory. In the first half of the 20th century, an era of vigorous development in physics, through the research of scientists such as Einstein, Schrödinger, Dirac, and Heisenberg, a comprehensive quantum theory gradually emerged, and quantum mechanics entered a new era.

In the era of modern quantum mechanics, the term "quantum" represents more properties rather than physical quantity. It encompasses uncertainty, wave-particle duality, superposition, and other quantum effects. It can even be directly understood as wave-particle duality, which is the fundamental characteristic of the quantum world. The concept of wave-particle duality was proposed by Louis de Broglie in 1924 based on Einstein's "photon" hypothesis. De Broglie suggested that if light, as a wave, can also be a particle, then particles can also be waves. For example, electrons can be waves. Therefore, like light, all matter exhibits wave-particle duality.

Unlike Newtonian mechanics, which describes the macroscopic world, quantum theory describes microscopic particles. Thus, humanity has finally gained a profound understanding of the world in which we exist.

1.2   Quantum Mechanics from Old to New

Although Planck's proposal of the quantum hypothesis successfully brought people into the world of quantum, as the founding father of quantum physics, Niels Bohr, said, "Anyone who is not confused by quantum theory has not understood it." For humans, the quantum world remains mysterious and unfamiliar. For this reason, quantum mechanics attracts countless scientists who strive to explore and unveil the truth about the microscopic world. In this process, the theory of quantum mechanics has also transitioned from the old to the new quantum mechanics period, gradually becoming a refined theory that can govern the microscopic world and bring about surprising applications.

1.2.1 Old Quantum Mechanics Period

Returning to Planck's quantum hypothesis, there were mainly two theories regarding blackbody radiation before Planck proposed the quantum hypothesis. One was Wien's formula, which approached the problem from the perspective of the particles' Boltzmann motion and reflected the discrete nature of objects. However, Wien's formula only matched experimental tests in the short-wavelength range and failed in the long-wavelength range. The other was the Rayleigh-Jeans formula, derived from Maxwell's theory of electromagnetic radiation, emphasizing energy continuity. Although it matched experimental data in the long-wavelength range and compensated for the shortcomings of Wien's formula, it lost the advantages of Wien's formula in the short-wavelength range.

To resolve these issues, Planck employed interpolation, combining Wien's and Rayleigh-Jeans' formulas to obtain a formula that perfectly matched experimental results. This is the famous Planck formula.

At the end of 1900, Planck proposed an explanatory solution for his formula. On December 14 of the same year, he presented his bold hypothesis in an article titled "On the Theory of the Energy Distribution Law of Normal Spectrum" to the German Physical Society. He suggested that the energy of an oscillator is not continuously variable but can only take integer multiples of a certain minimum value, which is directly proportional to the oscillator's frequency.

The proportionality constant h, known as the Planck constant, was obtained by fitting experimental data. Through this assumption, Planck derived his formula.

Since the electromagnetic oscillators can only absorb or emit electromagnetic waves with frequencies that match their frequencies, the idea that the energy of these oscillators can only take discrete values also implies that the emission and absorption of energy in blackbody radiation occur in discrete portions, known as "energy quanta." Simply, the electromagnetic waves emitted from a blackbody cannot be emitted continuously but in discrete portions, each referred to by Planck as a "quantum." Thus, the preliminary concept of quantum mechanics was introduced, and Planck successfully opened the door to quantum mechanics for humanity. December 14 is also known as "Quantum Day." As the founder of quantum mechanics, Planck was awarded the Nobel Prize in Physics in 1918, and asteroid 1069 was named after him.

Certainly, Plank was only the beginning of quantum mechanics, and he did not provide further physical explanations for this quantization hypothesis. He believed it to be a mathematical means of deriving a theory that would align with experimental data across the entire wavelength range. Soon, Einstein would refine and develop Plank's quantum theory.

In 1905, Einstein published "On a Heuristic Viewpoint Concerning the Production and Transformation of Light." In this article, Einstein boldly postulated that light is composed of discontinuous "energy quanta" or "photons." He proposed that photons have zero mass at rest but gain mass in motion. However, the concept of "photons" differed from Newton's "particles" in that Newton regarded light as solid particles, while Einstein's "photons" were quantized.

Through further research, Einstein discovered that when photons strike a metal plate, the electrons on the plate absorb the energy carried by the photons. Suppose the process absorbs too much energy, causing the electrons to exceed the binding energy of the atomic nucleus. In that case, the electrons break free and escape to the surface of the metal plate. This is known as the "photoelectric effect." Einstein's explanation elucidated why the energy of photoelectrons is solely dependent on the frequency of light and independent of its intensity. Even though the intensity of the light beam may be weak, a sufficiently high frequency will generate high-energy photons that facilitate the escape of bound electrons. Conversely, despite the intense intensity of a light beam, if its frequency is too low, it will not produce any high-energy photons capable of liberating bound electrons.

With the discovery of the "photoelectric effect," Einstein was awarded the Nobel Prize in Physics in 1921. It was through Einstein's work that we gained a deeper understanding of light. Einstein's quantum explanation of the photoelectric effect extended Plank's quantum theory and laid the foundation for Danish physicist Niels Bohr's atomic theory.

Before Bohr's work, there had been some research on atomic radiation. Specifically, in 1911, based on experiments on the scattering of alpha particles, Rutherford proposed the planetary model of atomic structure. According to the planetary model, electrons also revolve around the atomic nucleus, like planets orbiting the sun. However, according to classical electromagnetic theory, as electrons move around the nucleus, they emit electromagnetic waves and gradually lose energy, spiraling inwards toward the nucleus. This contradicted the actual observations, and Rutherford's planetary model of atomic structure quickly failed.

Figure 2   The planetary model of atomic structure

Therefore, in 1913, based on Rutherford's model, Bohr introduced the concept of quantized orbits for electrons outside the nucleus. He proposed that electrons do not have fixed orbits but appear randomly in specific regions. Bohr's atomic model resolved the stability issue of atomic structure. Subsequently, he developed a comprehensive theory of atomic structure.

Bohr summarized the work of his predecessors and concluded that the energy absorbed and released by electrons in atoms exists in a state of discrete energy quanta. Correspondingly, the potential energy positions that electrons can occupy in an atom must also be discrete, and these positions are called energy levels. The movement of electrons between energy levels is referred to as transition or electron transition. Since electrons cannot exist outside these energy levels, they do not fall onto the atomic nucleus, avoiding catastrophic annihilation. Bohr's theory successfully rescued the nuclear model of the atom and extended the concept of discretization to the subatomic realm.

Although Bohr's theory had difficulty providing a perfect explanation for helium atoms or atoms with a higher number of nuclear charges, it marked significant progress in the development of quantum science. From Planck's blackbody radiation formula to Einstein's photon hypothesis in the study of the photoelectric effect and then to Bohr's analysis of atomic spectral patterns, leading to the quantum theory of hydrogen atoms, quantum science continued to evolve. These theories can be regarded as early or old quantum theories.

However, the old quantum theory was merely a mixture of classical theories and quantization conditions, and there were still challenges in fully explaining the motion of microscopic particles. In fact, during these twenty years, physicists made limited progress, and most discussions revolved around the "quantum nature" of energy: energy is quantized, radiation is quantized, and electrons are confined to discrete energy levels.

Scientists realized that this newly emerged theory required fundamental changes and even alterations to basic assumptions. Thus, a revolutionary transformation of quantum mechanics began to take shape.

1.2.2 Innovations of Quantum Mechanics

After its embryonic stage, quantum mechanics rapidly experienced explosive development. In just four years, from 1924 to 1927, a group of talented, diligent, courageous, and diverse young physicists, without any coordinated organization, collectively established the fundamental concepts and theoretical framework of quantum mechanics. Finally, the dawn of a new era in theoretical physics began to emerge. In the quest for the laws governing the microscopic realm, quantum mechanics was established from two different paths, ushering in a brand-new era in physics. The discovery of bosons and fermions, the wave-particle duality hypothesis, matrix mechanics, and wave mechanics became the cornerstones of the new stage of quantum mechanics, propelling its further development.

Bosons and Fermions

The first person to discover the quantum indistinguishability of microscopic particles was the Indian physicist Satyendra Nath Bose. In 1921, Bose was recruited by Dhaka University with a lucrative offer to establish a physics department. There, Bose wrote the paper that would make him famous throughout history.

In his derivation, Bose introduced a revolutionary concept that photons are identical and indistinguishable. Based on this concept and utilizing Planck's proposed light quanta, Bose provided the correct derivation of the blackbody radiation formula for the first time in human history. Bose's breakthrough was astounding. Before this, no one had realized the fundamental difference between quantum and classical physics. Einstein translated Bose's paper into German and arranged for publication in a German journal.

Not only that, but Einstein immediately generalized this concept. Since photons are identical and indistinguishable, other particles must be the same. Einstein predicted the famous Bose-Einstein condensation phenomenon, and in 1995, physicists verified Einstein's prediction using ultracold atomic gases.

Meanwhile, three young geniuses also began to focus on this issue independently of Bose and Einstein. They were Wolfgang Pauli, Enrico Fermi, and Paul Dirac. Pauli published his first paper two months after graduating from high school at 18. In this paper, he studied general relativity. Fermi was one of the few physicists who excelled in both theory and experimentation. On the other hand, Dirac was introverted, reserved, and unwilling to interact with others, but this did not hinder his research.

In 1922, Bohr visited Göttingen and gave a series of lectures on how to use quantum theory to explain the arrangement of the periodic table. Despite progressing, Bohr still couldn't solve the biggest challenge: why don't electrons accumulate in the lowest energy level? This question troubled Pauli. After more than three years of thinking and research, inspired by the work of others, Pauli finally clarified this problem in 1925.

Pauli believed that to explain the periodic table. Two assumptions had to be made: first, in addition to spatial degrees of freedom, electrons also have a strange degree of freedom; second, no two electrons can simultaneously occupy the same quantum state. The first assumption was quickly confirmed, and the strange degree of freedom turned out to be spin. The second assumption is now known as the Pauli exclusion principle.

In contrast to Pauli, Fermi had been contemplating the distinguishability of electrons since 1924. Bohr and Sommerfeld's quantum theory failed to explain the spectrum of helium atoms. Fermi hypothesized that the main reason was that the two electrons in a helium atom are completely identical and indistinguishable. Still, he didn't know how to proceed with a quantitative discussion until he saw Pauli's article.

In 1926, Fermi published two papers consecutively. In these papers, Fermi described a new quantum gas in which the particles are identical and indistinguishable, and each quantum state can be occupied by at most one particle. This differs from the discussion of identical particles by Bose and Einstein, which the author has yet to mention before, where multiple particles can occupy the same quantum state. Several months later, Dirac used a new method to reexamine this problem and systematically presented the properties of identical particles.

Now we know that microscopic particles can be divided into two categories: bosons and fermions. Photons, hydrogen atoms, and others are bosons, while electrons, protons, and others are fermions. Bosons obey Bose-Einstein statistics: multiple bosons can occupy the same quantum state, while fermions obey Fermi-Dirac statistics: a quantum state can be occupied by at most one fermion.

The Hypothesis of Wave-Particle Duality

At the end of 1924, de Broglie proposed the "matter waves" hypothesis based on Einstein's "photon" hypothesis. De Broglie believed that if light, which is a wave, can also exhibit particle-like behavior, then particles can also exhibit wave-like behavior. For example, electrons can be considered as waves. Therefore, just like light, all matter possesses wave-particle duality. In his doctoral thesis, de Broglie conducted extensive quantitative discussions around this viewpoint.

First, he argued that if a particle has a momentum of p, then its wavelength is $\lambda = h/p$. Second, he proposed that since electrons are waves, they would form standing waves around protons. Following this thought, de Broglie miraculously derived the hydrogen atom's orbitals and energy levels, originally formulated by Bohr. Finally, de Broglie predicted that electrons would also undergo scattering and interference phenomena. Subsequently, scientists confirmed the wave-like nature of electrons through electron diffraction experiments.

The hypothesis of wave-particle duality, stating that all matter possesses this dual nature, shook the academic community. Particles and waves are fundamentally different forms of matter, and according to classical physics, they should not be able to merge. However, Einstein appreciated the hypothesis and stated, "A corner of the great curtain has been lifted." All subatomic particles can be partially described in terms of particles and partially described in terms of waves. The classical concepts of "particles" and "waves" lose their ability to completely describe the laws governing the motion of microscopic particles. Based on this understanding, Bohr proposed the famous "complementarity principle."

Matrix Mechanics

While the wave-particle duality challenged traditional theories, Heisenberg and Born were making groundbreaking progress in another direction of quantum theory. As we know, Bohr's theory successfully rescued the atomic nucleus model, but it struggled to explain helium atoms or atoms with more nuclear charges. Bohr tried various approaches, including changing the shape of orbits (energy levels) and temporarily abandoning energy conservation as universally valid in the microscopic world. However, these attempts did not adequately solve the problem.

Therefore, Heisenberg deeply reflected on the fundamental aspects of the problem. He believed that the key to failure lay in introducing too many concepts that had no meaningful position in actual observations. Concepts like "orbits" and "orbital frequencies" had no place in physical experiments. Thus, he proposed eliminating these unobservable quantities and transforming Bohr's theory based on concepts derived solely from meaningful experimental data. Heisenberg noticed that while orbits (energy levels) were not directly observable, the energy absorbed or emitted during a transition from one energy level to another had direct experiential meaning. These data could be filled into a two-dimensional table, which evolved into observable quantum mechanics quantities. Specific operations could be performed on these tables. In effect, this introduced matrices and their operations into the field of subatomic physics.

In September 1925, Heisenberg published "Quantum-Theoretical Re-interpretation of Kinematic and Mechanical Relations." This paper was of milestone significance. In the paper, Heisenberg wrote that its purpose was to "establish the foundations of quantum mechanics, which will include only relations between observable quantities." Subsequently, Born, Jordan, Dirac, and others refined and systematized Heisenberg's method mathematically. This marked the birth of matrix mechanics, which directly contributed to the development of the modern quantum mechanics framework.

In matrix mechanics, the two physical quantities, position and momentum, are no longer represented by numbers but by a huge table (matrix). In this way, position times momentum is no longer equal to momentum times position, and Bonn and Jourdan even calculated the difference between these two products. This eventually prompted Heisenberg to derive the famous "uncertainty relation," which shows that the deviation of experimental measurements of momentum and position cannot be arbitrarily small simultaneously. When the position is measured very precisely, the deviation of the measurement of momentum is bound to be larger, and vice versa.

Wave Dynamics

Schrödinger completed the new quantum mechanics' last and extremely important stroke, inspired by de Broglie's wave-particle duality.

On January 27, 1926, the academic journal *Annalen der Physik* received a manuscript from Schrödinger. In this manuscript, Schrödinger presented his famous wave equation (the Schrödinger equation) and wave function. He used these equations to provide the correct energy levels of the hydrogen atom. Schrödinger's wave equation for matter waves provided a theoretical framework for the systematic and quantitative treatment of atomic structure problems. Besides explaining the magnetic properties of matter and their relativistic effects, in principle, it can explain all atomic phenomena, making it the most widely applied formula in atomic physics.

In late 1926, the seemingly very different matrix mechanics and wave dynamics were soon shown to be mathematically equivalent. Schrödinger first proved the equivalence of wave mechanics and matrix mechanics, and then Dirac further unified matrix mechanics and wave mechanics through transformation theory. At this point, the theoretical system of quantum mechanics was initially created.

1.3 Mysteries of Quantum Mechanics

As quantum mechanics continued to develop, it brought more astonishing phenomena and more mysteries for scientists. Among these mysteries, physicists gradually formed two factions: the Copenhagen interpretation led by Bohr, Born, Heisenberg, Pauli, and Dirac, and the opposing faction led by Einstein and Schrödinger. It was through the continuous debates and experimental verifications between these two factions that the quantum theory was further refined.

1.3.1 The Uncertainty Principle and Schrödinger's Cat

In the history of quantum mechanics, 1927 is often cited as the end of the quantum mechanical revolution. In March of that year, Heisenberg proposed the uncertainty principle; in September of the same year, Bohr proposed the complementarity principle. In today's prevailing interpretation of quantum mechanics, the complementarity principle is rarely mentioned. Still, the uncertainty principle or the uncertainty relation remains an important and indispensable element for understanding quantum mechanics.

Among them, Heisenberg's interpretation of the uncertainty principle, known as Heisenberg's "gamma-ray microscope experiment," is particularly significant. This interpretation is often regarded as the "derivation" or "proof" of the uncertainty relation. Still, it was a thought experiment conceived by Heisenberg from his philosophical standpoint, serving as a semantic interpretation of the implications of the formal system of quantum mechanics.

Inspired by Einstein's idea that "the theory determines what we can observe," Heisenberg attempted to understand the electron's trajectory in a cloud chamber. Since matrix mechanics denies the existence of precise electron orbits, it becomes impossible to simultaneously observe the electron's exact position and momentum.

To address this, Heisenberg designed the famous "gamma-ray microscope experiment." According to his reasoning, to precisely observe the position of an electron, one must use high-energy gamma rays. However, high-energy gamma rays inevitably introduce significant momentum disturbances to the electron. Conversely, low-energy photons cause less disturbance to the electron's momentum but cannot precisely measure its position.

In simple terms, Heisenberg's uncertainty principle states that particles cannot simultaneously possess definite position coordinates and corresponding momenta objectively. At a given moment, an electron may be located at any point in space, with different probabilities for different positions. In other words, the electron's state at that moment is a superposition of states at all fixed points in space, known as the electron's quantum "superposition state." Each fixed point represents an "eigenstate" of the electron's position.

For example, in quantum theory, the electron's spin is explained as an intrinsic property, and no matter from which angle you observe the spin, you can only obtain two eigenstates: spin up or spin down. On the other hand, the superposition state is a probabilistic combination of eigenstates, and there can be infinitely many combinations of the two probabilities. The superposition state of an electron being both "up" and "down" is a fundamental rule that particles in quantum mechanics follow. Light also exhibits superposition states. For instance, in polarization, the electromagnetic field of a single photon oscillates in both vertical and horizontal directions. Hence, the photon is in a state of being both vertically and horizontally polarized.

However, when we measure the state of a particle (such as an electron), the superposition state of the electron no longer exists. Its spin is either up or down. To explain this process, Heisenberg introduced the concept of wave function collapse, which means that in the instant of observation by an observer, the initially uncertain "wave function" of the electron suddenly collapses into a specific position's "wave function." Therefore, quantum entities possess unmeasurable characteristics.

The superposition state of quantum severely contradicts our everyday experiences. As a result, in opposition to the Copenhagen interpretation of quantum mechanics, Schrödinger proposed a thought experiment involving a cat, known as "Schrödinger's cat," which has become widely known today.

Schrödinger postulated a scenario where a cat is confined in a box with poisonous gas. The switch of determining whether the toxic gas being released is a radioactive atom. In this experiment, the poison gas will be released if the radioactive atom decays, causing the cat to die. Whether the atom decays or not is unknown; to find out if the cat is dead, we can only open the box and observe. However, before we open the box, the cat is in a superposition state of being alive and dead. But the question is, a cat can only be dead or alive; how can it be both dead and alive?

Although a real cat cannot be dead and alive, the behavior of electrons (or atoms) is such. This experiment again placed Schrödinger in opposition to his established theory, leading some physicists to jest at him, saying, "Schrödinger didn't understand Schrödinger equation."

Despite Schrödinger's opposition, the belief in quantum superposition states has become firm since the birth of quantum computing in the 1980s. Quantum computers are the most prominent application of quantum superposition states.

1.3.2 God Does Play Dice

According to the principles of quantum mechanics, similar to gambling, the world itself is a game of chance. All matter in the universe is composed of atoms and subatomic particles, and probability rather than determinism governs these particles. This theory suggests that nature is built upon randomness, which contradicts human intuition. Therefore, many people find it difficult to accept, including Einstein.

Einstein found it incredibly challenging to believe that the essence of the real world is determined by probabilities, to the extent that he famously said, "God does not play dice." It is Einstein's disbelief that sparked a century-long debate about quantum mechanics.

Einstein and Bohr, pioneers and founders of quantum mechanics, held opposing interpretations of the theory, engaging in heated debates.

Einstein's viewpoint can be summarized by his statement, "God does not play dice." He emphasized that quantum mechanics cannot have non-local effects, meaning he insisted on the "locality" of classical theory. Einstein believed that three fundamental assumptions of classical physics—conservation laws, determinism, and locality—should apply to both classical and quantum mechanics. Conservation laws refer to the principles that certain physical quantities in a system do not change over time, such as energy conservation, momentum, and angular momentum. Determinism suggests that starting from classical physical laws, one can obtain definite solutions, such as determining the position of an object at a given moment using Newtonian mechanics.

Locality, also known as local realism, posits that forces can only influence a specific object in its immediate vicinity. In other words, the interaction between two objects must propagate through waves or particles as mediators. According to the theory of relativity, the speed of information transfer cannot exceed the speed of light, so an event occurring at one point cannot immediately affect another. Therefore, Einstein referred to instantaneous interactions between two particles as "spooky action at a distance." It is worth noting that classical physics before quantum theory also adhered to the principle of locality.

On the other hand, Bohr believed that measurement could change everything. He argued that particle properties are uncertain before measurement or observation. For instance, in the double-slit experiment, electrons can appear within a probability range in almost any predicted location until a detector precisely detects their positions. Only at the moment of observation the uncertainty of their positions vanishes. According to Bohr's principles of quantum mechanics, the act of measurement itself forces the particle to abandon its potential locations and choose a definite position—the one we observe. It is the act of measurement itself that compels the particle to make this choice.

Bohr believed that the nature of the real world is inherently fuzzy and uncertain. However, Einstein disagreed. He believed in the determinism of things and that they exist regardless of measurement or observation. Einstein famously said, "I think that whether or not the moon is there, the moon is always there." Thus, Einstein was convinced that quantum theory was still incomplete, lacking a description of the detailed characteristics of particles, such as their positions when unobserved. However, at the time, hardly any physicists shared his views. Despite Einstein's continuous questioning, Bohr remained steadfast in his perspective. When Einstein repeated the phrase "God does not play dice," Bohr responded, "Don't tell God what to do."

1.4 The Debate of Quantum Mechanics

1.4.1 Einstein's "Entanglement"

In the debate between Einstein and Bohr, an attempt to prove the absurdity of quantum mechanics finally materialized in 1935. Einstein and his colleagues Podolsky and Rosen published a paper titled "Can Quantum Mechanical Description of Physical Reality be Considered Complete?" It later became known as the EPR paper, named after the initials of the three authors. The arguments presented in this paper are referred to as the EPR paradox or Einstein's local realism. In this paper, Einstein introduced a powerful concept named "quantum entanglement" by Schrödinger.

Einstein devised a thought experiment describing the case of an unstable large particle decaying into two smaller particles, A and B. The large particle splits into two identical smaller particles, each acquiring kinetic energy and flying off in opposite directions. If particle A's spin is up, particle B's spin must be down to conserve the overall spin, and vice versa.

According to quantum mechanics, before measurement, the two particles should exist in a superposition state, such as a superposition of "A up, B down" and "A down, B up," each with a certain probability (e.g., 50%). Then, when we measure particle A, its state collapses instantaneously. If A collapses into the "up," B's state must be "down" due to conservation.

However, if a vast distance separates A and B, such as several light-years, according to quantum theory, B should also have an equal probability of being up or down at the moment of A's collapse. How is it possible for B to always choose the down state precisely when A collapses? Is there some way for A and B to communicate instantaneously? Even if they can somehow perceive each other, the signal between them would need to traverse thousands of light-years instantly, surpassing the speed of light, which goes against existing knowledge of physics. Therefore, Einstein believed that this constituted a paradox.

After reading the EPR paper, Schrödinger wrote a letter to Einstein in German, where he first used the term "Verschränkung" (entanglement) to describe the lingering correlation between two temporarily coupled particles in the EPR thought experiment.

Bohr responded to the EPR paradox as well. He believed that since the two particles form an entangled whole, describing the system using a wave function is only meaningful. They should not be regarded as two separate entities physically distant from each other. Since they are a coordinated entity, there is no need for any information to be transmitted between them.

Of course, Einstein did not accept Bohr's peculiar explanation, and the disagreement between the two persisted until their deaths, with no definitive resolution reached.

1.4.2 The Rectification of Quantum Entanglement

To rectify the true nature of quantum entanglement, we need to start with "Bell's inequality." Einstein and his supporters believed that the randomness of quantum entanglement was merely superficial, suggesting the existence of hidden variables behind it. Bell supported this viewpoint and attempted to experimentally prove Einstein's hidden variables hypothesis.

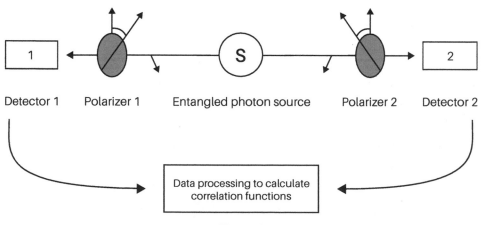

Detector 1   Polarizer 1   Entangled photon source   Polarizer 2   Detector 2

Data processing to calculate correlation functions

Figure 3

Bell proposed an experiment depicted in figure 3. According to local realism, the polarization directions of these photons are predetermined, and the measurement of one photon's polarization should be independent of the measurement outcome of the other photon. However, in quantum mechanics, measuring one photon's polarization inevitably affects the measurement outcome of the other photon.

For instance, we conduct four experiments where the polarizers on the left and right sides are set at angles of (0°, 0°), (30°, 0°), (0°, −30°), and (30°, −30°), respectively. In the first case, all the photons can pass through the polarizers. In the second and third cases, polarizers on each side are selected independently. In the fourth case, both polarizers on both sides are rotated. In simple terms, if the measurement outcome of one photon is independent of the measurement outcome of the other photon, then the result of both polarizers on both sides being rotated should be less than or equal to the sum of the results obtained when each polarizer is rotated separately. This is the essence of Bell's inequality. However, according to quantum theory, measuring one photon's polarization will inevitably affect the measurement outcome of the other photon, resulting in cases where the result of both polarizers being rotated exceeds the sum of the results obtained when each polarizer is rotated separately.

In other words, if the inequality holds, Einstein would be victorious, but if the inequality is violated, Bohr would prevail. Thus, Bell's inequality transformed the thought experiment from Einstein's EPR paradox into a tangible and feasible physical experiment. Although Bell intended to support Einstein by finding hidden variables in quantum systems, the results derived from his inequality did not support Einstein's theory.

Finally, in 1946, physicist John Wheeler became the first to propose an experiment using photons to realize entangled states. Specifically, light is a wave that has a particular direction of oscillation. Just as we observe water waves vibrating up and down while propagating forward, light also vibrates up and down in its oscillation direction. Ordinary natural light is a mixture of light rays with various oscillation directions. However, when natural light passes through a polarizer set in a specific direction, the oscillation direction of light becomes restricted, resulting in "polarized light" that only vibrates along a certain direction.

For example, the lenses of polarized sunglasses are polarizers. A polarizer can be imagined as having polarizing slits in a specific direction that only allows light vibrating in that direction to pass through. In contrast, most of the light vibrating in other directions is absorbed.

In the laboratory, scientists can use polarizers to measure and manipulate the polarization direction of light. Light can have different linear polarization directions, and perpendicular polarization directions can be analogous to the spin states of electrons. Therefore, the entangled states described using spin also apply to photons with slight modifications.

In other words, if the polarized light's polarization direction aligns with the polarizer's axis, the light can pass through; if the direction is perpendicular to the polarization axis, the light cannot pass through. If they form a 45° angle, half of the light can pass through while the other half cannot. However, in quantum theory, light exhibits both wave and particle properties. In the laboratory, it is possible to reduce light intensity by emitting individual photons.

It's important to note that individual photons also carry polarization information. When a single photon enters a polarizer, there are only two possible outcomes: pass or not pass. Therefore, when the polarization direction of the incident photon forms a 45° angle with the polarization direction of the polarizer, each photon has a 50% chance of passing through and a 50% chance of not passing. If this angle is different from 45°, the probability of passage will be another angle-dependent value.

This means that photons can exhibit entanglement while carrying the easily measurable property of polarization. Therefore, scientists can design experiments using photons to test Einstein's proposed EPR paradox. Leveraging the characteristics of photons, John Wheeler pointed out that a pair of photons generated after annihilating a positive and negative electron should have two different polarization directions. Shortly after, in 1950, Wu Jianxiong and Shaknov published a paper announcing the successful realization of this experiment, confirming Wheeler's idea and generating the first pair of entangled photons with opposite polarization directions in history.

1.4.3 Quantum Entanglement Today

When two strangers far apart have the same thought simultaneously, as if an invisible thread is connecting them, this phenomenon is known as "telepathy." Quantum entanglement is similar to this. It refers to the entangled relationship between two microscopic particles with a common origin in the microscopic world. These entangled particles can be likened to a pair of twins with telepathic abilities. No matter how far apart they are, whether on the scale of kilometers or even farther, when the state of one particle changes, the state of the other particle changes instantly. In other words, regardless of the distance between the two particles, as long as the state of one particle changes, it immediately induces a corresponding change in the state of the other particle.

On October 4, 2022, at 05:45 p.m. Beijing time, the Nobel Prize in Physics was announced. It was awarded to French scholar Alain Aspect, American scholar John Clauser, and Austrian scholar Anton Zeilinger. They were honored for "conducting experiments with entangled photons, disproving Bell's inequalities, and pioneering quantum information science." This year, the Nobel Prize in Physics was awarded to these three physicists because their pioneering research laid the foundation for quantum information science and recognized the field of quantum mechanics and entanglement theory.

One of the laureates, Professor Clauser, developed John Bell's ideas and conducted an actual quantum entanglement experiment. He built a device that emitted two entangled photons, each directed toward a polarizing filter for detection. In 1972, with his doctoral student Stuart Freedman, he demonstrated results that violated Bell's inequalities and were consistent with the predictions of quantum mechanics. The purpose of experimentally testing Bell's inequalities was to verify the existence of hidden variables in quantum systems and determine whether quantum mechanics is local or non-local.

However, Clauser's experiment still had some limitations—one of them being the low particle preparation and capture efficiency. Additionally, due to the predetermined settings and fixed angles of the polarizing filters, there were loopholes. Subsequently, Professor Aspect further refined this experiment by switching the measurement settings after the entangled particles left the source, ensuring that the settings present during particle emission would not affect the experimental results.

Furthermore, Professor Zeilinger began using entangled quantum states through precise tools and a series of experiments. His research team also demonstrated a phenomenon known as "quantum teleportation," which made it possible for quantum information to move from one particle to another over a certain distance.

From the proposal of Bell's inequalities to the first experiments conducted by Clauser and others to the subsequent supplementation and verification of loopholes, more than 50 years have passed. All of these Bell tests support quantum theory and indicate the failure of local realism. The long-term research efforts of these three physicists have ultimately rectified quantum entanglement, and the significance of this discovery for modern technology cannot be underestimated. Thus, the century-long debate between Einstein and Bohr has finally concluded.

1.4.4 The Significance of Quantum Entanglement

Despite being one of the most debated aspects since the inception of quantum mechanics, quantum entanglement has been confirmed. It has become a powerful tool in quantum physics, even though it deviates from everyday life experiences. Einstein referred to it as "spooky action at a distance," while Schrödinger considered it the most important feature of quantum mechanics.

Entangled quantum states can potentially become new means of storing, transmitting, and processing information.

Interesting things occur when particles in an entangled pair travel in opposite directions, and one of them interacts with a third particle in a way that creates entanglement. They enter a new shared state where the third particle loses its identity. Still, its original attributes are transferred to the particle left unentangled from the previous pair. This method of transferring an unknown quantum state from one particle to another is called quantum teleportation. Such experiments were first conducted by Anton Zeilinger and his colleagues in 1997.

It is worth noting that quantum teleportation is the only way to transfer quantum information from one system to another without losing any part of it. It is impossible to measure all the properties of a quantum system and send the information to a recipient who wants to reconstruct the system. This is because a quantum system can simultaneously contain several versions of each property, each with a certain probability of appearing in a measurement. Only one version remains once a measurement is made—the one read by the measuring instrument. The other versions have disappeared, and it is impossible to know anything about them. However, completely unknown quantum properties can be transferred intact to another particle through quantum teleportation, but the cost is that these quantum properties are destroyed in the original particle.

Once this was proven in experiments, the next step was to use two pairs of entangled particles. If one particle from each entangled pair is somehow entangled together, the two particles from the original entangled pairs that were undisturbed also become entangled, even though they have never interacted with each other. Anton Zeilinger's research team first demonstrated this entanglement swapping in 1998.

A pair of entangled photons can be sent in opposite directions through optical fibers and serve as signals in a quantum network. The entanglement between two pairs of photons extends the distance between nodes in such a network. The distance that photons can travel through optical fibers is limited because they can be absorbed or lose their characteristics if it becomes too long. Ordinary light signals can be amplified but entangled photon pairs cannot. Amplifiers would need to capture and measure the light, which would break the quantum entanglement. However, entanglement swapping means it is possible to further transmit the original state, reaching previously impossible distances.

Furthermore, quantum entanglement also holds importance in everyday life, primarily due to the mysterious interaction between entangled quantum particles. This interaction is somewhat similar to what we commonly refer to as the connection between twins. We know that twins have many similarities, such as height, appearance, temperament, and habits. This similarity extends beyond the consistency of cells in the biological realm. Daily, we are aware of a seemingly stronger telepathic connection between twins.

We, ourselves, and others are like two quantum entities. When one changes, the other undergoes a corresponding change, as if we can perceive others' thoughts. In quantum entanglement, the entanglement between two particles causes one to change in response to the other, regardless of how far apart they are. This mutual perception persists. It can be said that the mystery and marvel of quantum entanglement have opened the doors to a new world where we discover the unknown and redefine and understand the world.

1.5   Quantum and Technology

Although Einstein originally proposed quantum entanglement to challenge Bohr's interpretation, he probably didn't anticipate that more and more experiments would later confirm the correctness of quantum mechanics.

Since the 1930s, quantum mechanics has intersected and merged with disciplines such as nuclear science, informatics, and materials science, giving rise to the quantum technology revolution. As we enter the 21st century, the applications of quantum mechanics in computation, communication, and measurement are becoming increasingly abundant. These technologies have already been widely adopted, greatly facilitating societal progress. We are witnessing the acceleration of an era of quantum technology.

1.5.1 The Wave of Quantum Technology

We already know that quantum refers to the fundamental units that make up matter, the indivisible particles such as photons and electrons. Quantum mechanics studies and describes the structure, properties, and interactions of these fundamental particles in the microscopic world. Together with relativity, it forms the two foundational theories of modern physics.

In the mid-20th century, with the vigorous development of quantum mechanics, the first wave of quantum technology emerged, led by modern optics, electronics, and condensed matter physics. This wave gave birth to groundbreaking technological breakthroughs, such as lasers, semiconductors, and atomic energy, which laid the foundation for the formation and development of the modern information society.

For example, we often see advertisements for laser treatments that remove blemishes and unwanted body hair. With a laser, spots vanish from our faces, and hair falls off our arms. Behind this lies the application of principles related to quantum mechanics. As we know, the matter is composed of atoms with a nucleus at the center and electrons moving in fixed orbits around it. Electrons in different orbits have different energy levels. To illustrate, when we climb stairs while carrying a heavy load, we feel more tired climbing ten flights than climbing five. The higher floors require more energy expenditure, converted into gravitational potential energy. In other words, a heavier object on the tenth floor inherently possesses more energy than a similar object on the fifth floor. The same principle applies to launching rockets from Earth. The more fuel we consume during the launch, the farther we can send the rocket into space on a trajectory with greater inherent energy. The atomic world follows the same rules. We need more energy to move an electron to a higher orbit. In other words, an electron in a higher orbit inherently possesses higher energy.

Like any other light, lasers are composed of photons, each carrying a certain amount of energy. Common light, such as sunlight, generally contains many photons with varying energy levels. However, lasers are unique in that each photon within them carries the same amount of energy. This is the most significant distinction between lasers and ordinary light.

We have mentioned earlier that electrons in different orbits have different energy levels. At the same time, each type of laser photon has a specific energy. When a laser hits the skin, if the energy of the electrons in the skin does not match the energy of the laser photons, the skin will not absorb that particular laser. Conversely, if the energies match, the laser will be absorbed. This is the working principle behind laser blemish removal. When a laser is directed at the face, the electrons in healthy skin do not match the energy of the laser photons, so the skin remains undamaged. However, the electrons in dark spots match the energy of the laser photons, leading to absorption of the laser and eventual destruction of the blemishes.

Another example is semiconductor technology, which has already found extensive applications in our lives. For instance, our smartphones, televisions, and computers all contain essential components made of semiconductors. So, what exactly is a semiconductor? As people already know, atoms have electrons, which, under certain conditions, can break free from the binding force of the atomic nucleus and move freely within certain materials. This phenomenon gives rise to electric current.

Let's imagine the moving electrons as cars and the material they traverse as a road. It is easy to understand that the magnitude of electric current, or how fast the cars move, depends on the road conditions. Some materials have excellent road conditions, allowing cars to move swiftly without significant hindrance. These materials are called conductors. Most metals, such as copper, aluminum, and iron, are conductors.

On the other hand, some materials have terrible road conditions, full of obstacles blocking cars from moving. These materials are called insulators. Examples of insulators include ceramics, rubber, and glass. However, there are some special materials with peculiar road conditions. They have numerous obstacles that would typically impede cars from moving. But if external conditions change, such as increased temperature, the cars can start moving on the road again. These special materials are called semiconductors. This strange behavior occurs due to quantum mechanics. Semiconductor technology is based on the band theory derived from quantum mechanics, which explains and guides the understanding of solid-state physics and some important conclusions in quantum mechanics.

The essence of semiconductor electronic devices lies in controlling the transport of charge carriers using an electric field based on controlling the carrier concentration at different temperatures. The physical cores of semiconductor electronic devices vary among different types of devices but typically involve PN junctions and MOS contacts. The control of carrier concentration in PN junctions and MOS contacts is explained and guided by the band theory in solid-state physics, which is established based on the rules of quantum mechanics and can be calculated. Various useful electronic components can be created by utilizing the characteristics of semiconductors, with the most important ones being diodes and transistors. A diode has a unique property: when a voltage is applied in one direction, it allows current flow, while applying voltage in the opposite direction does not result in current flow. It is similar to a one-way street in a city: you can drive along it in one direction but not in the other. What is the use of a diode? It can play the role of a switch in an electrical circuit.

LED, short for Light-Emitting Diode, was invented by Isamu Akasaki, Hiroshi Amano, and Shuji Nakamura, who were awarded the Nobel Prize in Physics in 2014. LED lights are a special type of diode that can emit light. There are several advantages of using LEDs. First, they have very high luminous efficiency, much higher than traditional incandescent bulbs, making them highly energy efficient. That's why many stores, such as IKEA, sell LED bulbs. Second, LEDs have a long lifespan, lasting over ten times longer than incandescent bulbs. These advantages have led people to believe that LEDs will become the mainstream light source in the future.

However, due to limited observation and manipulation capabilities of microscopic physical systems, although the first wave of quantum technology brought many surprising applications, the main technological features of this stage were based on understanding and utilizing the laws of microscopic physics, such as energy level transitions, stimulated radiation, and chain reactions. Still, the observation and manipulation of physical media remained at the macroscopic level, such as current, voltage, and light intensity.

As time passed and we entered the 21st century, with the deepening understanding, research, and development of quantum mechanics principles, as well as the continuous improvement of observation and manipulation capabilities of microscopic physical systems, the second wave of quantum technology, characterized by precise observation and control of micro-particle systems using unique quantum properties such as superposition and entanglement, is on the horizon.

The evolution of quantum technology is expected to change and enhance how humans acquire, transmit, and process information, providing a strong driving force for the evolution and development of future information societies. Quantum technology will merge with information science disciplines such as communication, computation, and sensing, forming a new field of quantum information technology.

Quantum technology is primarily applied in three major areas: quantum computing, quantum communication, and quantum measurement. It has demonstrated the potential to overcome classical technological bottlenecks in improving computational processing speed, information security capabilities, measurement precision, and sensitivity. Quantum information technology has become one of the focal points in the evolution and industrial upgrading of information and communication technologies, with significant fundamental and disruptive impacts on national scientific and technological development, emerging industry cultivation, national defense, and economical construction.

1.5.2 Prospects of Quantum Technology

Today, the information technology revolution, particularly the accelerated breakthroughs, and applications of emerging information technologies such as artificial intelligence (AI), quantum information technology, blockchain, and 5G, is driving humanity's transition from a material-based society to a knowledge-based society. In a knowledge-based society, the importance of information surpasses that of material, becoming humanity's most valuable strategic resource. The thirst for information has reached unprecedented levels, and traditional technologies based on classical physics can no longer meet the demands of information acquisition, transmission, and processing, leading to three major technological challenges.

First, computing power approaches its limit. In the era of big data, on the one hand, the data collected by humans is growing explosively. Still, the storage capacity for such massive data is limited by traditional means. On the other hand, the development of AI technology demands higher computing power, which traditional computers struggle to provide due to the limitations of Moore's law. Although supercomputing can be achieved through hardware stacking, the potential for improvement in computing power is extremely limited, and it consumes a tremendous amount of energy.

Second, information security is vulnerable. Traditional information encryption techniques are built on the complexity of computation. However, with the advancement of computing power, such encryption systems can theoretically be cracked, even including blockchain, which is currently based on computational foundations. Information security still has certain vulnerabilities and risks.

Third, the precision of information is hard to enhance further. Traditional classical measurement tools no longer meet the demand for precision in various fields. Increasingly, more precise measurements are needed in areas such as time standards, medical diagnosis, navigation, signal detection, scientific research, etc. There is an urgent need for new technologies to overcome the current technological limitations.

In the face of the challenges presented by current information technology, quantum technology based on quantum mechanics shows unique advantages and provides new solutions to overcome the bottleneck of traditional classical technology development.

First, quantum computers will break through the bottleneck of computing power. Quantum computing, based on quantum bits as the basic unit, achieves data storage and computation through the controlled evolution of quantum states, possessing tremendous information-carrying and ultra-parallel processing capabilities that classical computing cannot match. The leap in computing power brought by quantum computing has the potential to become a "catalyst" for accelerating technological advancements in the future. Once a breakthrough is made, it will greatly impact fundamental scientific research, the development of new materials and medicine, information security, and AI, among many other areas in the economic and social domains. Its development and application play a significant role in national scientific and technological development, industrial transformation, and upgrading.

Second, quantum communication will overcome the bottleneck of communication security. The quantum state of microscopic particles possesses inherent unclonability, meaning that any attempt to steal information would disrupt the original information and be detected by the receiver. Therefore, quantum communication ensures the non-reproducibility and unbreakability of information at the physical-principle level, thus achieving absolute security in communication. Quantum communication, based on the principles of quantum mechanics to guarantee information security or key transmission, mainly consists of QT and QKD. The research and development of quantum communication and quantum information networks will bring about significant changes and impacts in fields such as information security and communication networks, becoming one of the focal points in the technological development and evolution of the information and communication industry.

Finally, quantum precision measurement breaks through the bottleneck of measurement accuracy. Compared to traditional measurement techniques, quantum precision measurement technology enables a leap in measurement accuracy. Quantum measurement relies on the precise measurement of microscopic particle systems and their quantum states, accomplishing the transformation and information output of physical quantities of the measured system. It has significant advantages over traditional measurement techniques regarding accuracy, sensitivity, and stability. It is widely applied in various fields, including time standards, inertial measurement, gravity measurement, magnetic field measurement, target recognition, etc. Quantum physical constants and quantum measurement technology have become important references for defining basic physical quantities and measurement standards. In the future, quantum measurement is expected to be at the forefront of applications in fields such as biological research, medical diagnostics, and new-generation positioning, navigation, and timing systems for aerospace, national defense, and commercial applications.

With the continuous progress of science and technology, quantum technology will lead to a new technological revolution. It will gradually affect all aspects of social development, driving humankind into the era of quantum civilization.

Application Section

MEETING QUANTUM TECHNOLOGY

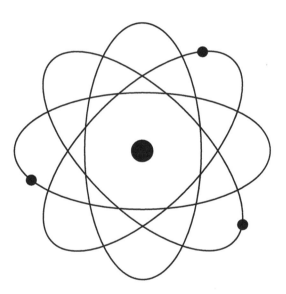

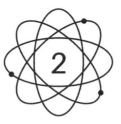

QUANTUM COMPUTING

2.1 Introduction

In 1900, Planck first proposed the concept of energy quantization in his paper, kicking open the door to quantum mechanics. In the quantum world, all matter can be reduced to 61 fundamental particles, with the heaviest being a mass no greater than 3.1×10^{-25} kg.

In the 1940s, Turing defined the meaning of algorithms and described what we now call the Turing machine: a single universal programmable computing device capable of executing any algorithm. Subsequently, computers gradually evolved into an industry and profoundly transformed our lives.

In 1981, renowned physicist Feynman observed the numerous difficulties encountered by classical computers based on the Turing model when simulating quantum mechanical systems. He proposed the idea of simulating quantum systems using classical computers. When quantum physics and computing met at a crossroads, the concept of a universal quantum computer emerged in 1985.

Since then, quantum mechanics has entered a rapid transformation into a genuine societal technology, and the pace of human progress on the path of quantum computing applications has accelerated. Today, quantum computing is no longer far from our reach.

2.1.1 From Classical Computing to Quantum Computing

As is well known, classical computers use bits as units of information storage, each representing either 0 or 1 using binary notation. However, in quantum computing, everything changes. Quantum computers employ quantum bits (qubits) as information units, and a qubit can represent both 0 and 1 simultaneously.

Furthermore, due to the property of superposition, a qubit in a superposed state can be nonbinary that interacts during the computation, achieving a state of being both 1 and 0 at the same time. This characteristic allows quantum computers to superpose all possible combinations of 0 and 1, enabling the simultaneous existence of states for 1 and 0. This feature theoretically grants quantum computers capabilities several times greater than those of classical computers in certain applications.

In classical computers, a 2-bit register can store only one binary number at a time, whereas a 2-qubit register in a quantum computer can simultaneously maintain the superposition of all four states. When the number of qubits is n, a quantum processor operating on n qubits is equivalent to performing 2^n operations on classical bits. This greatly enhances the processing speed of quantum computers.

However, according to quantum mechanics, energy is quantized in the microscopic world, like continuously magnifying a slope under a microscope and discovering that all slopes are composed of small levels. Quantum is not a specific particle; it refers to the phenomenon of energy quantization in the microscopic world. After undergoing "measurement," a quantum system collapses into a classical state. This is the thought experiment of the classical "Schrödinger's cat." When we open the sealed container, the cat is no longer in a superposition but exists in a unique state, either dead or alive. Similarly, after each measurement following quantum algorithm operations, a quantum computer will obtain a uniquely determined result, which may vary with each measurement.

Furthermore, due to another strange quantum property called entanglement, even if quantum bits are physically separated, the behaviors of two or more quantum objects remain interconnected. According to the laws of quantum mechanics, this pattern remains consistent in millimeters, kilometers, or astronomical distances. When a quantum bit is in a superposition between two basic states, ten qubits utilizing entanglement can exist in a superposition of 1,024 basic states.

Unlike classical computers, the computational power of quantum computers grows exponentially with the increase in qubits. It is this capability that endows quantum computers with extraordinary abilities to simultaneously process a large number of results. In an unobserved superposition state, n qubits can contain the same information as 2^n classical bits. Therefore, 4 qubits are equivalent to 16 classical bits, which may sound like a minor improvement. However, 16 qubits are equivalent to 65,536 classical bits, and the number of states contained in 300 qubits exceeds all the estimated atoms in the universe—an astronomical figure.

This exponential effect is why people are so eager for quantum computers. It can be said that the greatest characteristic of quantum computers is their speed. Take prime factorization as an example. Every composite number can be expressed as a multiplication of several prime numbers, with each prime number being a factor of that composite number. Expressing a composite number in the form of prime factorization is called factorizing. For example, 6 can be factored into the prime numbers 2 and 3. However, prime factorization becomes a complex mathematical problem when the number becomes large. In 1994, researchers took the help of 1,600 high-end computers and spent eight months factorizing a 129-bit number successfully. But with the use of a quantum computer, it would only take one second to crack it.

2.1.2 Crafting Quantum Algorithms

Just like classical computing, quantum computing also requires following specific algorithms. Similar to how ordinary algorithms are designed to support conventional computers in problem-solving, quantum algorithms are designed for ultra-fast quantum computers. Quantum algorithms not only fulfill the infinite potential of quantum computing but also bring new possibilities for AI.

As we already know, unlike classical computers, the information unit in quantum computing is a quantum bit. The most distinctive feature of a quantum bit is that it can exist in a superposition state of 0 and 1, meaning a quantum bit can simultaneously store both 0 and 1 data. In contrast, a traditional computer can only store one of them. For example, a 2-bit quantum memory can store four data: 00, 01, 10, and 11, whereas a traditional memory can only store 1.

In other words, an n-bit quantum memory can simultaneously store 2^n data, and its storage capacity is 2^n times that of traditional memory. Therefore, a quantum computer composed of 10 qubits has computational power equivalent to a 1,024-bit classical computer. And for a quantum computer composed of 250 qubits (n = 250), the amount of data it can store exceeds the number of atoms in the universe. In other words, even if all the atoms in the universe were used to build a traditional classical computer, it would still be inferior to a 250-qubit quantum computer.

However, it has always been a formidable challenge to connect these qubits, write programs for quantum computers, and compile their output signals in a way that harnesses their supercomputing capabilities. It was not until 1994 when Peter Shor of Bell Laboratories proposed a quantum algorithm that effectively factorizes large numbers, reducing the difficulty of factorization from exponential to polynomial time.

The current widely used computer encryption scheme, RSA encryption, relies on the time complexity of prime factorization. It would take several years to factorize a large integer using the fastest algorithms available today. However, with Peter Shor's algorithm, a quantum computer with sufficient qubits can easily break any large integer under the RSA model. Peter Shor was awarded the Gödel Prize, the highest award in theoretical computer science, in 1999 for his achievement.

According to Peter Shor's estimates, using today's most efficient algorithms, it would take millions of years for traditional computers, even if all the computers in the world worked together, to factorize a 250-bit number. However, a quantum computer can accomplish this task in just a few minutes. When a quantum computer factors a 250-bit number, it performs parallel computations on the order of 10 to the power of 500. This revolutionary breakthrough in quantum computation implies that quantum computers can perform calculations and trigger extensive research in quantum computing and information.

Soon after Peter Shor developed the first quantum algorithm, in 1996, Lov Grover of Bell Laboratories claimed to have discovered an algorithm for efficiently searching and sorting databases. This algorithm enables lightning-fast searches in unstructured data. While ordinary search algorithms typically take time proportional to the number of items n to be searched, the complexity of Grover's algorithm is only n^{-2}. Therefore, if the data size is increased by 100, the time required for a conventional algorithm to perform the search would also increase by 100, while Grover's algorithm would only require ten times the original time.

2.1.3 Quantum Algorithms Today

Most quantum computations are performed in what is known as quantum circuits. A quantum circuit is a series of quantum gates operating on a quantum bit system. Each quantum gate has inputs and outputs and performs operations similar to hardware logic gates in classical digital computers. Like digital logic gates, quantum gates are connected sequentially to implement quantum algorithms. Quantum algorithms, as algorithms running on quantum computers, utilize the unique properties of quantum mechanics, such as superposition or quantum entanglement, to solve specific problem statements.

In addition to Shor's algorithm and Grover's algorithm, the main quantum algorithms today also include Quantum Evolutionary Algorithms, Quantum Particle Swarm Optimization, Quantum Annealing Algorithm (QAA), Quantum Neural Networks (QNN), Quantum Bayesian Networks, Quantum Wavelet Transform, and Quantum Clustering Algorithm (QC). A comprehensive catalog of quantum algorithms can be found on the Quantum Algorithm Zoo website.

Quantum software is a collective term referring to the complete set of instructions for quantum computers, ranging from hardware-related code to compilers, circuits, all algorithms, and workflow software.

Quantum annealing is an alternative model for circuit-based algorithms as it is not built with gates. "Annealing" is a heat treatment process for metals where the metal is slowly heated to a certain temperature, held there for a sufficient amount of time, then cooled at a suitable rate. The purpose is to reduce metal's hardness, improve machinability, stabilize dimensions, reduce deformation and crack tendencies, and eliminate structural defects. In short, "annealing" addresses the issue of unstable hardware processes in material development, while "quantum annealing" tackles the problem of suboptimal solutions in mathematical computations like combinatorial optimization.

Quantum annealing is implemented through superconducting circuits, coherent Ising machine with laser pulses, and coherent quantum computing based on simulated annealing (SA), along with digital circuits like Field-

Programmable Gate Arrays (FPGA) to realize quantum algorithms. Quantum annealing starts with the quantum superposition state of all possible states (candidate states) with equal weights in a physical system. It undergoes quantum evolution following the time-dependent Schrödinger equation.

Quantum tunneling occurs between different states due to the time-dependent strength of the transverse field, causing continuous changes in all candidate states and achieving quantum parallelism. When the transverse field is finally turned off, the expected system solves the original optimization problem, which corresponds to the ground state of the corresponding classical Ising model. In the case of optimization problems, quantum annealing utilizes quantum physics to find the minimum energy state of the problem, which is equivalent to the optimal or near-optimal combination of its components.

An Ising machine is a non-circuit alternative specifically designed for optimization problems. In the Ising model, the energy from the interaction between each pair of electron spins in a collection of atoms is summed up. Since the energy depends on the alignment of the spins, the total energy of the collection depends on the direction of each spin point. The general Ising optimization problem is determining the spin states to minimize the system's total energy. Using the Ising model for optimization requires mapping the parameters of the original optimization problem to a representative set of spins and defining how the spins interact with each other.

Hybrid computing typically involves converting a problem (such as optimization) into a quantum algorithm where the first iteration is run on a quantum computer. While it can quickly answer, it is only a rough evaluation of the effective solution space. Then, a powerful classical computer is used to find the exact solution, which requires examining a subset of the original solution space.

2.2   Quantum Supremacy

In 2019, Google made the first announcement of achieving "quantum supremacy," bringing quantum computing into the public eye and igniting a wave of excitement in quantum computing. The following year, in 2020, a Chinese team announced the development of the quantum computer "Jiuzhang," challenging Google's claim of achieving quantum supremacy and establishing global computational leadership. Jiuzhang, with 76 photons and 100 modes, demonstrated a processing speed for "Gaussian boson sampling" that was a million trillion times faster than the fastest supercomputer, Fugaku. For the first time in history, the performance of a photon-based quantum computer surpassed that of the fastest classical supercomputer in terms of computation speed.

Furthermore, Jiuzhang was also effectively a hundred billion times faster than Google's prototype of a 53-qubit superconducting quantum computer named "Sycamore," which was announced the previous year. This breakthrough made China the second country in the world to achieve quantum supremacy and pushed forward the next milestone in quantum computing research.

As Jiuzhang became a globally significant scientific achievement, let's explore what "quantum supremacy" means and what it entails.

2.2.1 The Introduction of Quantum Supremacy

Quantum supremacy is not a term with political connotations as implied by its name; rather, it is a purely scientific term used to describe when a quantum computer surpasses the computational capabilities of the strongest existing classical computers for a specific problem, referred to as "quantum advantage" or "quantum supremacy."

In 2019, Google announced the first achievement of quantum supremacy. According to their research paper, the Google team named their quantum computer "Sycamore." It focused on solving a problem roughly understood as "verifying the randomness of a quantum random number generator." Sycamore consists of a chip with 53 qubits. It can perform a million samplings of a quantum circuit in just 200 seconds, while the same computational task would take around 10,000 years on Summit, the world's largest supercomputer. If we compare 200 seconds to 10,000 years as the best performance from both sides, it signifies the overwhelming advantage of quantum computing over supercomputing. Thus, this work is considered a milestone in the history of quantum computing as it demonstrated quantum supremacy in an experimental environment, as recognized by *Nature*.

Quantum supremacy was originally defined by John Preskill from the California Institute of Technology as the point at which a quantum computer can perform tasks beyond the reach of any available classical computer. It is often seen as the most advanced supercomputing achievable on classical architectures. Initially, it was estimated that a quantum computer with 50 or more qubits would be able to demonstrate quantum supremacy. However, some scientists argue that it depends more on how many logical operations (gates) can be executed in a quantum bit system before coherence decays, as errors increase significantly after coherence decay, making further computations infeasible. Additionally, the connectivity of qubits is also crucial in this context.

This made IBM researchers formulated the Quantum Volume (QV) concept in 2017. A larger QV implies a more powerful computer, but increasing the number of qubits alone does not increase the QV. QV is a hardware-agnostic performance metric considering several factors for gate-based quantum computers, including the number of qubits, qubit connectivity, gate fidelity, crosstalk, and circuit compilation efficiency.

At the end of 2020, IonQ announced a QV of four million for its fifth-generation quantum computing. Before this, Honeywell's 7-qubit ion trap quantum computer had the highest publicly reported QV of 128, followed by IBM's 27-qubit superconducting quantum machine with a QV of 64. In July 2021, Honeywell claimed to achieve a QV of 1,024 with an updated version of their System Model H1, the highest QV experimentally measured to date.

In addition, a year after Google announced achieving quantum supremacy, in 2020, a team of Chinese scientists developed "Jiuzhang," which further advanced upon the "Sycamore" achievement. The realization of "Sycamore" quantum supremacy depends on the number of samples. While "Sycamore" only takes 200 seconds to collect one million samples, the Summit supercomputer takes two days. Quantum computing demonstrates superiority compared to supercomputers in this scenario. However, if 100 billion samples are collected, classical computers only need two days, while "Sycamore" would require 20 days to complete such a large sample collection. Under these conditions, quantum computing loses its advantage.

However, the quantum computational advantage of "Jiuzhang" for solving the Gaussian boson sampling problem does not depend on the number of samples. Moreover, in terms of equivalent speed, "Jiuzhang" is even 100 billion times faster than "Sycamore" on the same track. According to the current best classical algorithm, "Jiuzhang" takes 200 seconds to collect 5,000 samples, while using China's "Sunway TaihuLight" would require 2.5 billion years, and even the world's top-ranked supercomputer "Fugaku" would need 600 million years.

Furthermore, in terms of state space, "Jiuzhang" exhibits an advantage with an output quantum state space of scale 10^{30}, far surpassing "Sycamore." It can be said that the outstanding performance of "Jiuzhang" firmly establishes China's leading position in international quantum computing research and represents a significant achievement in quantum computing.

2.2.2 Classical Computing and Quantum Computing

Based on the quantum superposition, many quantum scientists believe that quantum computers will far surpass any classical computer in specific tasks. However, achieving quantum supremacy is still an ongoing battle.

The reason behind this lies in the conditions required for achieving quantum supremacy. Scientists believe that quantum supremacy becomes possible when the number of manipulable qubits exceeds a certain threshold. This involves two key points: the number of manipulable qubits and their precision. Only when both conditions are met can the superiority of quantum computing be realized.

However, whether it is the "Sycamore" with 54 qubits achieving quantum supremacy or the "Jiuzhang" quantum computing prototype with 76 photons, although the number of manipulated qubits is continuously increasing, researchers still face challenges regarding the precision of quantum computing and the significant potential of supercomputing engineering.

One crucial aspect is the coherence time of qubits, which refers to the duration in which qubits can maintain their quantum state. The longer the qubits can maintain a superposition state (where qubits represent both 1 and 0 simultaneously), the more program steps they can handle, enabling more complex computations. However, when qubits lose coherence, information is lost. Therefore, quantum computing technology must also address how to control and read qubits and perform quantum error correction operations on the quantum system after achieving high fidelity in reading and control.

At the same time, classical computing algorithms and hardware are continually being optimized, and the potential of supercomputing engineering cannot be underestimated. For example, IBM claims that simulating a 53-qubit, 20-depth quantum random circuit sampling can be accomplished by classical simulation in just over two days or even better.

As mentioned earlier, realizing "Sycamore" quantum superiority relies on the number of samples. When collecting one million samples, "Sycamore" has an absolute advantage over supercomputers. However, when collecting 100 billion samples, classical computers still only need two days, while "Sycamore" would require 20 days to complete such a large sample collection, thus losing the advantage of quantum computing.

Moreover, for a long time, the superiority of quantum computers has been limited to specific tasks. For instance, Google's quantum computer targeted "random circuit sampling." Generally, when selecting such specific tasks, careful consideration is needed to ensure they are well-suited to existing quantum systems while being difficult to simulate for classical computers.

This implies that quantum computers do not surpass classical computers for all problems but only for certain specific problems where efficient quantum algorithms have been designed. For problems without quantum algorithms, quantum computers do not have an advantage.

This is where the creative breakthrough of "Jiuzhang" lies. The secondary demonstration of "quantum supremacy" by "Jiuzhang" not only proves the principle but also indicates that "Gaussian boson sampling" may have practical applications, such as solving specialized problems in quantum chemistry and mathematics. More broadly, mastering the ability to control photons as qubits is a prerequisite for building any large-scale quantum Internet.

In conclusion, whether it's in terms of the quantity or precision of quantum computing or the potential or limitations of classical computing, the competition between quantum computing and classical computing will be a long-term dynamic process.

From a layperson's perspective, some aspects of quantum physics may appear "without rhyme or reason" and seemingly incomprehensible. However, this is precisely the fascination of quantum mechanics and the meaning behind scientists' efforts. Interpretations of quantum mechanics can be understood as physicists attempting to find a "correspondence" between the mathematical theory of quantum mechanics and the real world. From a deeper perspective, each interpretation reflects a certain worldview.

People rejoice in every technological breakthrough, and it is in these efforts that human civilization can keep moving forward. Just as the quantum computer is named "Jiuzhang," the ancient Chinese textbook-like meaning from the *Nine Chapters on the Mathematical Art* (*Jiuzhang Suanshu*). It also holds people's imagination and aspirations for the future world.

2.3 The Significance of Quantum Computing

Quantum mechanics is a branch of physics that studies the behavior of subatomic particles. Quantum computers use mysterious quantum mechanics and transcend the properties of the limits of classical Newtonian physics. Using these computers has been a long-held dream of the technology to achieve exponential growth in computing power.

2.3.1 The Application of Quantum Computing

Before full-scale quantum computers become available, there are already some quantum computing applications. One prominent application is the combination of small-scale quantum computing with classical computing in hybrid quantum computing. Another application is the potential implementation of quantum-inspired computing algorithms on classical computer hardware. Quantum-inspired computing is based on the idea that a problem that is difficult to solve on a classical computer may become easier to solve by redefining it in a way inspired by quantum physics. However, the execution is still classical.

A practical distinction between classical computing and quantum computing is that if a solution utilizes the principles of superposition and entanglement in quantum mechanics, it can be called a quantum solution or at least a hybrid classical/quantum solution. If the solution does not utilize these phenomena, we would call it a classical solution, even if it may not resemble a typical classical computing solution.

Quantum-inspired computing can be implemented using standard computer hardware or specialized computer hardware. Typically, quantum-inspired software is also quantum-ready, meaning once the hardware becomes available, it can easily be ported to run on a true quantum computer. The software will become even more powerful when running on a true quantum computer.

Microsoft's quantum-inspired algorithms are designed to run on classical computers, and they have already been successful in use cases such as improving cancer detection in radiology scans. Microsoft claims that its quantum-inspired algorithms are "particularly useful for optimization problems—those involving sifting through vast numbers of possibilities to find the best or most efficient solutions—that are so complex they are beyond the reach of current techniques."

Microsoft also claims that by translating complex computational problems into quantum-inspired solutions, Azure can achieve several orders of magnitude performance acceleration. They have collaborated with Willis Towers Watson and financial services company Ally to explore how such algorithms can be applied in risk management, financial services, and investment domains.

Quantum Computing Inc (QCI) is another example of implementing quantum-inspired software on classical computer hardware. They offer a software platform called Qatalyst, which enables users to leverage the latest breakthroughs in quantum computing by running quantum-inspired software on classical computer hardware. One of their applications is the Quantum Asset Allocator (QAA), which uses quantum-inspired techniques to solve NP-hard problems that hinder optimal portfolio allocation. QCI claims that QAA can solve NP-hard problems, including cardinality and minimum buy-in constraints. The Qatalyst software is also quantum-ready and can be used when true quantum computers become available.

Toshiba's Simulated Bifurcation Machine is another example of implementing quantum-inspired techniques on standard computer hardware. It runs on general-purpose classical computers and claims to solve large-scale combinatorial optimization problems at high speed, outperforming SA methods by 100 times.

Fujitsu's Digital Annealer is an example of specialized computer hardware implementation. The hardware is "designed specifically to more efficiently solve larger and more complex combinatorial optimization (CO) problems."

2.3.2 The Possibilities of Quantum Computing

In early 2021, Forbes reported that leading quantum computing would be applied in various industries, including AI/machine learning, financial services, molecular simulation, material science, oil/natural gas, security, manufacturing, transportation/logistics, IT, and healthcare (pharmaceuticals). Furthermore, quantum computing offers enticing possibilities for future technological development, and researchers attempting to harness the power of this new hardware primarily focus on three types of problems.

The first type of problem involves analyzing the natural world, specifically simulating the behavior of molecules with a level of precision unmatched by today's computers. Computational chemistry is the largest application area in this regard. In the past two years, quantum computing has made increasingly significant contributions by replacing guesswork with empirical evidence.

For instance, simulating a relatively simple molecule like caffeine would require a conventional computer with 10^{48} bits, equivalent to 10% of the number of atoms on Earth. Simulating penicillin would require 10^{86} bits—larger than the universe's total number of observable atoms. Traditional computers cannot handle such tasks, but such calculations become possible in quantum computing. Theoretically, a quantum computer with 160 qubits can simulate caffeine, while simulating penicillin requires 286 qubits. This provides a more convenient means for designing new materials or finding better methods to improve existing processes.

On August 27, 2020, the Google Quantum Research Team announced the largest-scale chemical reaction simulation on a quantum computer. The achievement was featured on the cover of *Science* magazine with the title "Hartree-Fock on a Superconducting Qubit Quantum Computer."

To accomplish this milestone, researchers used the Sycamore processor to simulate the isomerization reaction of dinitrogenene, a molecule composed of two nitrogen and two hydrogen atoms. The quantum simulation matched the simulations performed by the researchers on classical computers, validating their work. It's worth mentioning that the Sycamore used in this new research is the same 54-qubit processor recognized by *Nature* as a milestone in the history of quantum computing. While this chemical reaction may be relatively simple and achievable without a quantum computer, it demonstrates the enormous potential of using quantum simulations to develop new chemical substances.

Moreover, quantum computing also holds promise for benefiting AI. Potential applications of quantum algorithms for AI include QNN, natural language processing, traffic optimization, and image processing. QNN, as a research field that combines quantum science, information science, and cognitive science, can utilize the powerful computational capabilities of quantum computing to enhance information processing in neural computation.

In natural language processing, in April 2020, Cambridge Quantum Computing announced a successful test of natural language processing on a quantum computer. This marked the first successful validation of quantum natural language processing applications worldwide. Researchers translated sentences with grammar into quantum circuits using natural language's "intrinsic quantum" structure. They processed the program on a quantum computer to obtain answers to questions within the sentences. Quantum computing holds the potential to achieve further breakthroughs in semantic awareness in natural language processing.

Last, quantum computing offers possibilities for optimizing complex problems that involve too many variables for today's computers to handle. For example, one application of quantum computing in complex problems is establishing better financial market models, strengthening encryption by inventing new digital currencies, and improving operational efficiency in chaotic and complex domains such as trade settlement and reconciliation. Derivative pricing, portfolio optimization, and risk management in highly complex and constantly changing situations are also tasks that quantum systems can handle.

2.3.3 The Significance of Quantum Computing

Even though the development of quantum computing faces many realistic and daunting challenges, quantum computing remains a potentially revolutionary technology that physicists and computer scientists have been dreaming of for decades. In addition to exploring more complex problems, the development of quantum computers has fundamentally brought an informational upgrade to human society, and the addition of quantum computing may help people process digital information faster and more securely in the future.

As we all know, three industrial revolutions have occurred in human history, the first being the steam age, the second being the electrical age, and the third being the information age. The third Industrial Revolution, dominated by computers, is now further evolving into the fourth Industrial Revolution with the Internet, big data, and AI as its beginning. In the third and fourth industrial revolutions, computers play an important leading role, and chips, the "brain" of computers, are the top priority in the technological revolution.

In 1965, Intel co-founder Gordon Moore predicted that the number of components that could fit on an integrated circuit would double every 18 to 24 months. Moore's law summarizes the speed of information technology progress. In the 50 years of Moore's law application, computers have entered millions of homes and become indispensable tools for most people, information technology has entered countless ordinary homes from laboratories, the Internet has connected the world, and multimedia audio-visual equipment has enriched everyone's life.

Moore's law is of great significance to the whole world. However, classical computers will eventually be physically limited to continue Moore's law with silicon transistors as the basic device structure. As computers evolved, transistors became smaller, making the intervening barriers thinner and thinner. At 3 nm, there are only a dozen atoms in the barrier. In the microscopic system, the electron will have a quantum tunneling effect, which cannot accurately represent 0 and 1, which is often said that Moore's law hit the ceiling of the reason.

Although researchers have also proposed the idea of replacing materials to enhance the barrier within the transistor, the fact is that no matter what material is used, there is no way to stop the electron tunneling effect. This difficult problem is a natural advantage for the quantum. After all, the semiconductor is the product of quantum mechanics; the chip is also developed after scientists understand the quantum properties of the electron.

In addition, based on the superposition characteristic of quantum, quantum computing is like the 5G in arithmetic power, which brings fast but also brings no change in speed itself. For example, AlphaGo, which defeated all humans in the Go, is the "soft growth" of the AI algorithm from its initial development to the final victory over the global champion. On the other hand, it is the "hard growth" of the computing power of the NPU running AlphaGo. The development of any one of the two elements may lead to the final result of AlphaGo becoming smarter.

Based on their powerful computing power, quantum computers can rapidly complete calculations that electronic computers cannot do. The growth in arithmetic power brought by quantum computing may even create the fourth wave of AI. The potential applications of quantum algorithms generated for

AI include QNN, natural language processing, traffic optimization, and image processing. Among them, QNN, a research field formed by the intersection of several disciplines of quantum science, information science, and cognitive science, can utilize the powerful arithmetic of quantum computing to enhance the information processing capability of neural computing.

Although quantum computing is not as versatile as traditional computing, it comes to us as a portal to a strange new world, a portal that allows us to see our current world with a revised definition. In the long run, with worldwide layout and development, quantum computing will most likely remove the time barrier completely, the cost barrier will be lowered, and a new machine learning paradigm may emerge. However, quantum computing will still need a long exploration process before a truly universal quantum computer with universal capabilities like traditional computers takes shape.

QUANTUM AI

3.1 Introduction

Quantum computing and AI have already become hot research topics in their respective fields.

With the continuous development of AI technology, it has become a strategic technology leading this round of technological revolution and industrial transformation, serving as a new engine driving economic and social development. AI is gradually being applied in various areas of social life, such as smart homes, intelligent healthcare, smart agriculture, intelligent manufacturing, fintech, and autonomous driving, and its industrialization has achieved remarkable results. Machine learning has demonstrated its advantages in many complex scientific problems, including cancer detection, extreme weather prediction, and exploration of exoplanets.

On the other hand, quantum computing has gradually become another powerful tool driving the progress of the digital society. Among numerous scientific achievements in the 20th century, quantum theory is undoubtedly one of the greatest discoveries, providing the framework for the establishment of various modern unified theories in physics. Compared to some incremental technologies in the current scientific community, quantum computing has a disruptive effect. It disrupts the prevailing electronic computing, where traditional mainstream computers still rely on electrons as the basic carriers. It can be said that quantum computing is one of the core contents of digital technology and the driving force behind the digital economic era.

What kind of future will be revealed when AI and quantum computing come together, when disruptions combine and overlap?

3.1.1 Quantum Computing AI

Quantum AI, as the name suggests, is the combination of quantum technology and AI, specifically referring to the application of quantum computing technology in AI.

Compared to the 70-year history of AI, quantum computing is relatively younger. Although quantum mechanics played a crucial role throughout the 20th century, directly leading to the development of information technologies such as semiconductor transistors and lasers, the concept of quantum computing truly emerged in the 1980s.

In 1981, the renowned physicist Richard Feynman observed the difficulties encountered by classical computers based on the Turing model when simulating quantum mechanical systems. He then proposed the idea of simulating quantum systems with classical computers. Since then, quantum mechanics has entered a rapid transformation into a genuine social technology, and the development speed in quantum computing applications has been increasing.

Generally speaking, quantum computing is a new computing paradigm that follows the laws of quantum mechanics to manipulate quantum information units for calculations, completely different from existing computing models. Classical computing uses binary digital electronic methods for calculations, where binary states are always in a definite state of 0 or 1.

In contrast, quantum computing leverages the superposition property of quantum mechanics, enabling the superposition of computational states. It includes not only 0 and 1 but also superposition states where 0 and 1 exist simultaneously. Additionally, with the feature of quantum entanglement, quantum computers theoretically possess faster processing speed and stronger processing power than classical computers using the most powerful algorithms in specific problems.

When quantum computing meets AI, the computational power of quantum computing will directly benefit the development and breakthroughs of AI. One major characteristic of AI's computational demand is the parallel computing of massive heterogeneous data, which is difficult for traditional CPU chips to handle, leading to the popularity of GPU, FPGA, ASIC, and other chips in AI.

However, quantum computing possesses parallel computing capabilities and information-carrying capacity that classical computing technology finds challenging. In the foreseeable future, although quantum computers will not completely replace classical computers, they will play a role in specific scenarios with high computational requirements based on their unique advantages in parallel computing and quantum behavior simulation. At the same time, the supercomputing power of quantum computing originates from quantum parallelism, which makes it very suitable for parallel computing required for AI. Conversely, smarter machine-learning algorithms must adapt as quantum computers are gradually introduced to the public. Therefore, the meeting of quantum computing and AI will inevitably promote the further development of quantum computing and AI.

3.1.2 The Combination of Quantum Computing and AI

Since Peter Shor published the first quantum algorithm, the factorization algorithm for large numbers, mathematicians and computer scientists have developed other quantum algorithms to solve problems difficult for classical computers to tackle. Many of these dozens of quantum algorithms are orders of magnitude faster than the most efficient classical algorithms known to us. However, these algorithms can only be implemented in the unique quantum environment they require.

Some of the most important work in quantum computing involves creating algorithms to simulate various quantum systems, ranging from laser technology to chemical and medical applications. These quantum algorithms are expected to surpass similar classical computations and endow quantum computers with tremendous computing power.

Currently, classical algorithms for molecular simulation are limited to the types of molecules they can simulate, usually to molecules with fewer than 70 spin orbitals. As the complexity of the simulation grows exponentially, it becomes increasingly challenging to handle. However, a single quantum bit (qubit) can effectively represent one of these orbitals, and a quantum computer with just 100 qubits would surpass classical computers in simulating molecules. These simulations could unveil previously unknown compounds and provide new therapeutic approaches for various diseases.

From depth-first search to adiabatic optimization, quantum algorithms have broad and continuously advancing applications. When these algorithms are put into practical use, some of the most frustrating, challenging, and exponentially complex problems in commerce, administration, medicine, and engineering will be solved effortlessly.

Quantum algorithms not only unlock the infinite potential of quantum computers but also bring new possibilities for AI. Based on principles such as superposition and entanglement, which are inherent to quantum systems, quantum algorithms are particularly suitable for solving optimization problems at the core of AI and machine learning. Since 2018, companies led by Google have begun investing in quantum AI, especially deep learning.

The Tensorflow Quantum (TFQ) framework proposed by Google in 2020 is a representative achievement in integrating quantum algorithms and AI. TFQ is an open-source library for hybrid quantum-classical machine learning. It allows researchers to design, train, and test hybrid quantum-classical models by simulating quantum processors' algorithms. These models can also be run on real quantum processors for the quantum part. TFQ can be used for quantum classification, control, approximate optimization, and other functionalities.

It can be said that AI and machine learning are key to the development of quantum algorithms. By combining quantum algorithms with AI, AI can rapidly acquire "intelligence" and quickly learn in human society. In terms of solving optimization problems and finding optimal solutions, it can surpass human capabilities within a few months.

IBM's theoretical work has shown that exponential acceleration can be achieved even with classical data in certain supervised machine-learning applications.

QC Ware has developed two types of data loaders, parallel and optimized data loaders, which convert classical data into quantum states for machine learning applications. They also utilize an optimized distance estimation algorithm.

Matthias Troyer from Microsoft proposes a general perspective of focusing on "small data, big computation" to avoid the "input bottleneck." For example, CQC has established a team to research quantum natural language processing. Hartmut Neven from Google has invented another unique yet subtle principle of quantum machine operation.

While quantum algorithms promise infinite prospects for computing, the current execution of quantum algorithms still lacks available quantum hardware—a quantum computer with a sufficient number of qubits and sufficient computational power to support these algorithms. Overcoming these hardware challenges is primarily a matter of technology, and the pathways to overcome these difficulties are clear. However, if quantum machine learning is to become a "killer application" for quantum computers, these challenges must be overcome, and they will ultimately be overcome.

3.1.3 The Disruption and Advancement of Quantum Computing and AI

If we say that machine learning, with the help of quantum computing's high parallelism, achieves further optimization of traditional machine learning, then the derived applications of quantum computing in AI will further push the boundaries of current AI applications.

For example, in AI, the application of game theory is becoming increasingly widespread, especially in distributed AI and multi-agent systems. When quantum expansion combines with game theory to form quantum game theory, it provides new tools for solving problems in the development of AI. Quantum game theory models the decision-making process of game phenomena and studies and describes them and their strategies using relevant methods from quantum mechanics. In 2016, DeepMind's AlphaGo, a subsidiary of Google, was born based on quantum game theory. In its first year, AlphaGo defeated world-class Go player Lee Sedol, and the following year it defeated the world number one, Ke Jie, taking AI to new heights.

Another example is in the semantic analysis of natural language, where there are certain similarities in the mathematical structures of both AI and quantum computing. In other words, quantum algorithms are highly suitable for simulating quantum systems. Ambiguity can be expressed through superposition, which means that quantum computing can significantly increase processing speed in natural language processing.

Furthermore, pattern recognition, such as object recognition, is an especially important field in AI. However, researchers in AI often only consider the recognition and differentiation of classical objects.

In recent years, with the continuous development and increasing attention to quantum computing, researchers have solved the problem of quantum gates and conducted research on quantum measurement resolution. It has been found that through optimal protocol design, rapid recognition can be achieved with the fewest queries, effectively demonstrating the resolution capability of quantum operations.

Of course, conversely, AI can also help solve complex quantum problems. For example, synthesizing drugs and handling different chemical reactions, which are difficult to simulate by solving quantum equations, can be addressed partially using AI methods. Another example is solving the ground state energy of quantum many-body Hamiltonians, which can also be achieved with the help of AI methods.

Whether it is applying quantum technology to AI to further promote the development of AI or applying AI to quantum technology to solve complex quantum problems, in the current context of Moore's law approaching physical limits, quantum computing as a disruptive technology is in urgent need of development.

Quantum computing takes quantum as the fundamental computing unit, revolutionizing the computing architecture based on electrons as the basic unit. First, it can enhance the security of information communication. Second, it can improve computational power for broader applications across various industries. It can be said that quantum computing is an important force in the digital technology system and a core force in the digital economy era alongside big data, AI, and blockchain.

Today, with the increasing research and development efforts and investments by major scientific research teams, research institutions, and technology giants, the field of quantum AI is showing signs of explosive growth. This drives the development of AI, improving the efficiency and accuracy of machine learning and promoting the prosperity of the quantum world. The future is driven by quantum computing and AI, and the world outlined by quantum AI is exciting and full of challenges.

3.2   Quantum Machine Learning

Nowadays, while traditional machine learning has gained widespread application in the business field, quantum machine learning is gathering new strength. This force is even more attention-grabbing than any other field of quantum computing because of the anticipated advantages of quantum technology.

3.2.1 Advantages of Quantum Machine Learning

First, quantum machine learning can accelerate computational speed. Quantum computing can offer a clear way to accelerate classical techniques. The HHL algorithm allows for a universal acceleration of linear algebra, but it only applies to native quantum data and outputs. The Grover algorithm, on the other hand, enables a universal quadratic speedup in many unstructured search applications. However, can these techniques truly be utilized in practice? The most challenging aspect of attempts to directly accelerate classical machine learning techniques is the requirement for effective data loading and superposition queries by quantum devices.

Second, quantum machine learning provides more computational space. Microsoft suggests that the field of quantum machine learning should set aside the big data problem and focus on the "small data, big computation" problem. Such problems seek benefits from large computational workspaces, which is something unique that quantum computers can provide due to the vast Hilbert space of qubit systems.

Xanadu points out that for recent QML (descriptive scripting language) approaches, many promising techniques are best understood as kernel methods in traditional machine learning. IBM claims that 2021 is a significant milestone as it provides a learning task example that can offer exponential acceleration but requires classical access to data. This involves building a series of data sets as a starting point, making it challenging to classify using traditional algorithms. Quantum computing is the kernel function for the classical support vector machine. IBM also published on quantizing QNN, the higher-dimensional tasks that can be achieved compared to comparable classical neural networks, and the role of intractable classical feature maps in affecting trainability. Pasqal released a specialized framework that leverages the reconfigurability of neutral atom devices to represent graph kernels.

Nonlinear differential equation systems are prominent problems that can be expressed concisely but require significant computational resources for numerical solving. Such equations appear in various scientific and commercial applications, to the extent that modeling complex processes is needed: from structural engineering to aerospace, chemistry to biology, finance to epidemiology. To address this, Qu&Co has developed a new technique for handling nonlinear differential equations on recent quantum computers, namely differentiable quantum circuits. This approach trains QNNs to utilize the large Hilbert space for handling derivatives. Qu&Co has also extended this method to stochastic differential equations. Moreover, Qu&Co has filed a patent application covering its technology.

Cambridge Quantum Computing has identified QNLP (Quantum Natural Language Processing) as a specific area within QML. In 2021, they reported their first experimental results. A data set containing 130 sentences and 105 noun phrases was encoded using a 5-qubit IBM device. QNLP leverages the expanded computational space provided by quantum computers. The remarkable similarities between the formalism proposed by Cambridge Quantum and the ZX calculus representation of quantum mechanics suggest a fruitful approach. Perhaps, as stated by Bob Coecke, Chief Scientist of Cambridge Quantum, "language is quantum-native."

Last, quantum machine learning can provide unique quantum data. An increasingly important focus is on cases where QML should surpass classical machine learning when the data set contains quantum correlations or interference effects that need to be addressed. Work in 2021 has begun to formalize and structure this, applicable to learning tasks and generative models.

Caltech published a study in 2021 defining the capabilities of different machine learning models. That one is traditionally driven by learning but uses measured outputs from quantum systems, e.g., physics experiments, simulated quantum simulators, or iterations of VQA; the other that maintains quantum coherence during learning. A key result is that classically driven ML can do very well and is comparable to full quantum learning regarding mean case prediction accuracy. Full quantum learning provides an exponential advantage for worst-case prediction accuracy.

Google believes that the most general form of support quantum can provide for advances in fields such as chemistry is not only theoretical simulations of systems but may also include the generation of quantum data sets for classically driven machine learning. A Quantum Circuit Boon Machine (QCBM) is a VQA that implements a generative model. Research published in 2021 demonstrated for the first time that a specific type of QCBM, the Ising Boon Machine, can perform sampling tasks that would be difficult for any classical computer.

3.2.2 AlphaFold and Protein Folding

Proteins are the most important biological molecules, and their physical shapes and how they interact with each other have a profound impact on biological functions and drug targeting, making it a highly researched problem. Solving the protein folding problem has always been a potential goal of quantum computing.

Levinthal's paradox states that a short protein could have 3,198 combinations of bond angles. However, once it forms a long chain, it adopts a unique preferred folding shape within milliseconds. However, trying out each combination sequentially would take longer than the lifetime of the entire universe.

This is the protein folding problem, or more precisely, a collection of related problems, including predicting the structure of simple proteins from amino acid sequences, understanding protein conformations, and understanding the dynamics of folding.

From the perspective of quantum mechanics, however, there is no paradox. It is simply a problem that classical computing finds difficult to solve but can be solved by a quantum computer.

AlphaFold, developed by DeepMind, a subsidiary of Google, uses traditional AI methods to solve the protein folding problem. The pharmaceutical industry has also indicated that drug development timelines can be significantly accelerated when this area receives proper attention. AlphaFold2 has improved the latest technology for predicting protein folding structures to 92.4%–95% GDT. For individual protein chains, it achieves reasonable accuracy in predicting structures over 90% of the time. This is also DeepMind's most remarkable success to date, and some even consider it the most significant achievement in AI so far.

However, Dr. Bhushan Bonde unveiled the hype and reality during his speech at Quantum Tech 2021. Traditional quantum chemical approximation techniques are crucial for screening compounds for drugs against COVID-19. However, they consume significant and impractical computational resources. His simulations often utilize the full GPU capabilities on Microsoft Azure cloud, run for weeks, and are still not fast enough. Replicating such experiments would have implications for energy consumption, heat management (cooling computer hardware), and, more importantly, time efficiency. Dr. Bonde also believes that the performance of AlphaFold has not truly aligned with the biology-related requirements of pharmaceutical companies, as they need accurate identification of the drug-binding pockets.

Dr. Bonde believes that future advancements in AI and quantum computing are complementary tools. Quantum computing provides a new tool for analytical solutions in quantum chemistry. It is also expected to be a driver for further improvement in the performance of future machine learning systems, particularly when quantum correlations are present in the data. In this regard, IBM has also been actively advancing quantum protein folding approaches, such as proposing a quantum resource-efficient variant of the variational quantum eigensolver (VQE), which has been used to "fold" problems on their early devices.

3.3 Quantum Computing Commercialization

Since Nobel laureate Richard Feynman first proposed the concept of quantum computing in 1981, stating that applying quantum mechanical effects could greatly enhance computational speed, quantum computing theory has been developing for over 30 years. In 1994, Bell Labs proved experimentally that quantum computers could perform logarithmic calculations at speeds far exceeding those of traditional computers. This marked the first successful experiment following the proposal of quantum computing theory. Subsequently, capital began to flow into quantum computing research, and the field gradually transitioned from the laboratory stage to the engineering application stage over the next decade.

3.3.1 Market Prospects of Quantum Computing

Currently, quantum computing is receiving increasing attention. As an emerging technology that breaks the limitations of Moore's law and enables exponential growth in computing power, it has attracted numerous technology companies and large academic institutions to invest in its development.

Although predictions of the quantum computing industry vary, almost all perspectives agree that its scale will be enormous. As Doug Finke, the operator of the quantum information tracking website "Quantum Computing Report," stated, "I believe the quantum computing market could reach US$1 billion by around 2025 and potentially US$5–10 billion by 2030." The latter value equals 10%–20% of today's high-performance computing market. According to Honeywell's estimation, the value of quantum computing over the next 30 years could reach US$1 trillion.

According to Boston Consulting Group's prediction, the conservative estimate is that the quantum computing market will reach US$2 billion by 2035. With increasing adoption rates, the market is projected to soar to US$260 billion by 2050. If the main limiting factor of quantum computing development is that the physical quantum bit error rate can be significantly reduced, the market size could reach US$60 billion by 2035 and increase to US$295 billion by 2050. In comparison, the current total size of the global commercial and consumer markets is US$800 billion.

Given the vast market prospects of quantum computing, it is not surprising that it has attracted significant public and private investments. Mainstream venture capital firms and large corporations have begun to invest heavily in private quantum computing companies. Companies like Google, IBM, and Honeywell invest heavily in quantum computing through various means, including in-house research, private equity investments, and collaborations. A recent report stated that in 2021 alone, over US$1 billion in private investment was used for quantum computing research.

Most of the projects and companies in this field are in the early stages, mainly in the seed or Series A funding rounds, and some are still in the incubation/acceleration phase. It is worth noting that the nature of investments in quantum computing is unique due to the supercomputing capabilities and encryption provided by quantum cryptography for communication networks. "National team investment" is indispensable in driving the field forward.

In fact, in addition to mainstream investment institutions and large companies, "national teams," such as the US Department of Energy, CIA, National Aeronautics and Space Administration (NASA), Canada's STDC, and Australia's Telecom, have played a significant role in promoting quantum computing research and commercialization through donations, investments, incubation, and other forms. For example, one of Google's quantum computing projects involves collaboration with NASA to apply the technology's optimization capabilities to space travel.

Furthermore, the US government is prepared to invest approximately US$1.2 billion in the National Quantum Initiative (NQI) program. The program was officially launched in late 2018 and provided an overall framework for quantum information science research and development in academia and the private sector. The UK's National Quantum Technology Program (NQTP) was launched in 2013 and pledged to invest £1 billion over ten years. Currently, the program has entered its second phase.

For China although Chinese technology companies entered the field of quantum computing relatively late compared to the US, industry-leading companies and research institutes have started to lay out their strategies in quantum computing in recent years. During the Two Sessions in 2021, quantum information technology was mentioned for the first time, becoming one of the core technologies for China's key breakthroughs in the 14th Five-Year Plan. It is also one of the seven strategic areas for "national security and comprehensive development."

In terms of technology giants, Tencent entered the field of quantum computing in 2017 and proposed the "ABC2.0" technological layout, which involves using AI, robotics, and quantum computing to build future-oriented infrastructure. Huawei has been engaged in quantum computing research since 2012. It has made it an important research area at the Huawei Central Research Institute's Data Center Laboratory, focusing on quantum computing software, quantum algorithms, and applications. Alibaba, on the other hand, has established laboratories to carry out hardware-centric full-stack development and is also building an ecosystem, exploring applications in collaboration with partners in the upstream, middle, and downstream of the industry chain.

Both technology companies and startups have high expectations and enthusiasm for quantum computing.

3.3.2 The Sino-US Competition in Quantum Computing

It can be said that quantum technology surpasses any technology currently possessed by any country in computing, including chip technology and blockchain technology, which has been widely discussed. Therefore, as one of the major challenges at the forefront of global technology, quantum computing has become a focus of competition between countries, especially China and the US.

The US is the country that first included quantum information technology in its defense and security research and development programs, and it is also the country that has made the fastest progress. As early as 2002, the US Defense Advanced Research Projects Agency (DARPA) formulated the "Quantum Information Science and Technology Roadmap." In June 2018, the US passed the "NQI Act," planning to allocate US$1.275 billion to the Department of Energy, the National Institute of Standards and Technology, and the National Science Foundation over ten years to fully promote the development of quantum science.

Regarding US companies, Google established its quantum computing project as early as 2006. In October 2019, Google announced in *Nature* that it achieved quantum supremacy using a 54-qubit processor called Sycamore. Specifically, Sycamore could perform a specific operation in 200 seconds, while the same computation would take approximately 10,000 years on the world's largest supercomputer, Summit. This work marked the first experimental demonstration of quantum supremacy in human history and was considered a milestone in the history of quantum computing by *Nature*.

In August 2020, Google simulated the largest-scale chemical reaction to date on a quantum computer. Google achieved accurate computational predictions of chemical processes by using quantum devices to perform Hartree-Fock calculations on molecular electronic energies and employing VQE for error correction. This indicates that Google has entered the second phase of developing quantum computers.

In addition to Google, in 2015, IBM published a paper in *Nature Communications* on a prototype quantum chip made of superconducting materials. In August 2020, IBM achieved a 64-qubit QV, a performance metric proposed by IBM to measure the power of quantum computers. In September, IBM released an ambitious roadmap, stating that by the end of 2023, they could build quantum hardware with 1,000 qubits.

Intel has been researching various qubits, including superconducting and silicon spin qubits. In 2018, Intel successfully designed, manufactured, and delivered a 49-qubit superconducting quantum computing test chip called Tangle Lake, which had a computational power equivalent to 5,000 the 8th-generation i7 processors. It allowed researchers to evaluate error correction techniques and simulate computational problems.

China has also been continuously increasing its investment in quantum technology. For China, quantum science is crucial if it wants to have a say in technology and achieve true technological advancement. According to the 14th Five-Year Plan, China has incorporated quantum information into its national strategic scientific and technological forces and strategic emerging industries. It accelerates the development of cutting-edge technologies such as quantum computing, quantum communication, neural chips, and DNA storage. It also promotes cross-disciplinary innovation between information science, life science, materials, and other basic disciplines.

China has made remarkable breakthroughs and achievements in quantum computing. In December 2020, China claimed to have achieved quantum supremacy for the first time. A Chinese scientific team created a quantum computer named "Jiuzhang" to complete a specific calculation in minutes. In contrast, the world's most powerful supercomputer would take billions of years to complete the same calculation.

Subsequently, China announced the successful development of the "Jiuzhang II" quantum computing prototype with 113 photons. According to the officially published theory of optimal classical algorithms, the "Jiuzhang II" is 1,024 times faster than the fastest supercomputer processing Gaussian boson sampling. Additionally, the 66-qubit programmable superconducting quantum computing prototype "Zuchongzhi II" achieved "quantum supremacy" in the superconducting system, surpassing the computational complexity of Google's "Sycamore" by six orders of magnitude.

Although there is still a distance to go from the laboratory to reality, the development of quantum science undoubtedly brings about a reconstruction of human civilization. Explorations of quantum entanglement, multidimensional space, and spacetime travel will update the current physics and the scientific concepts developed based on current physics. Just like space exploration, humans will eventually set foot on the moon.

3.3.3 Applying Challenges of Quantum Computing

The disruptive nature of quantum computing is foreseeable. However, there is still a long way to go before quantum computing can be fully integrated into practical production and daily life. As the technology is still in development, the industry faces the reality of technical breakthroughs and challenges in scaling production while transitioning quantum technology from academia to commercialization.

Currently, the commercialization of quantum computing is still in the stage of technological exploration. Although significant breakthroughs have been made in quantum computing at the theoretical and experimental levels, with countries such as the US, Europe, and China achieving different breakthroughs and achievements in quantum technology, there are only a few early-stage commercial applications in this field.

One reason is that building a quantum computer requires mastering and controlling superposition and entanglement. Without superposition, quantum bits (qubits) would behave like classical bits and could not exist in multiple states simultaneously to perform multiple computations. Without entanglement, even if qubits are in a superposition state, they would not generate additional insights through interactions, rendering computation impossible as each qubit's state would remain independent of others.

It can be said that effectively managing superposition and entanglement is the key to creating commercial value with qubits. The states of quantum superposition and entanglement, also known as "quantum coherence," involve the mutual entanglement of qubits, where a change in one qubit affects all other qubits. To achieve quantum computing, all qubits need to maintain coherence. However, the interaction between the quantum coherent entities and their surrounding environment leads to the rapid loss of quantum properties, known as "decoherence."

Typically, algorithm design aims to minimize the number of gates to complete the execution before decoherence and other sources of errors disrupt the results. This often requires a hybrid computing scheme that offloads as much work as possible from the quantum computer to classical computers. Scientists speculate that a truly useful quantum computer would require 1,000 to 100,000 qubits. However, skeptics of quantum computing, such as the renowned quantum physicist Mikhail Dyakonov, point out that the large number of continuous parameters used to describe the state of a useful quantum computer could be its fatal weakness. For example, a 1,000-qubit machine would require $2^{1,000}$ parameters to describe its state, which is about 10^{300}, a number greater than the number of subatomic particles in the observable universe. How can the errors of these 10^{300} continuous parameters be controlled?

According to scientists, the threshold theorem proves that this is achievable. They argue that as long as the error for each qubit of every quantum gate is below a certain threshold, infinitely long quantum computation becomes possible, albeit with a substantial increase in the number of required qubits. Additional qubits are needed to handle errors by forming logical qubits from multiple physical qubits. This is somewhat similar to error correction in current telecommunication systems, which use extra bits to verify data. However, this significantly increases the number of physical qubits that need to be addressed, as we can see, surpassing astronomical figures. This also highlights the magnitude of the technical problems that scientists and engineers must overcome.

For example, in a typical 3 V CMOS logic circuit used in classical digital computers, a binary 0 is any voltage measured between 0 V and 1 V, while a binary 1 is any voltage measured between 2 V and 3 V. If, for instance, 0.5 V of noise is added to the signal of binary 0, the measurement result will be 0.5 V, which still correctly indicates the binary value 0. Therefore, digital computers have strong resistance to noise.

However, for a typical quantum bit (qubit), the energy difference between 0 and 1 is only 10^{-24} joules (which is one billionth of the energy of an X-ray photon). Error correction is one of the biggest obstacles to overcome in quantum computing, and it is worrisome because it introduces significant overhead in auxiliary computations, making the development of quantum computers challenging.

In terms of commercialization, almost no companies in the quantum technology race have achieved cumulative profitability. Due to high technological barriers, companies invest billions of dollars in research and development, while their products are still undergoing constant trial and error, making commercialization difficult. Taking IonQ as an example, a unicorn company specializing in quantum computing, according to the company's financial data released, it generated revenues of US$200,000 and US$0 in 2019 and 2020, respectively, with net losses of US$8.926 million and US$15.424 million, indicating very low commercialization levels, with most of the investment being spent on research and development.

After tracking over 200 quantum technology startups, Douglas Finke predicts that the vast majority will no longer exist within ten years, or at least not in their current form. He stated, "There may be some winners, but there will also be many losers. Some will go out of business, some will be acquired, and some will be merged."

It can be seen that despite the series of breakthroughs achieved in current quantum computing technology and the continuous process of advancement, governments worldwide are highly attentive and have invested significant financial and human resources. However, truly scalable commercialization still has a long way to go. Scalable commercialization requires a demand for technological stability, fundamentally different from experimental and small-scale applications.

The core problem currently faced by quantum computing technology lies in the challenges of empirical physics. While theoretical physics has reached a basic level of maturity, when entering the empirical physics stage, we need to transform the elusive and highly unstable quantum entanglement into a controllable stability technology.

Overall, the future of quantum computing is optimistic. Everything regarding the commercialization of quantum computing has just begun. So far, we may have only discovered the tip of the iceberg in quantum computing. Whether the first practical application of quantum computing comes from a technology company, a bank, a pharmaceutical company, or a manufacturer attempting to apply this technology, the race for quantum computing has already begun.

QUANTUM COMMUNICATION

4.1 Introduction

From the inception of Bell Laboratories to the rise of Silicon Valley, and the advent of electronic computers and the ubiquitous Internet, human civilization has been gradually entering the era of information. However, conventional communication methods often rely on encryption to address security concerns. Yet, even encrypted codes are susceptible to being deciphered, especially with the emergence of quantum computing, which utilizes parallel processing to easily crack many current encryption methods.

Today, the transmission of information has shifted from "how to transmit" to "how to securely transmit." Quantum communication, as the direct successor of this information revolution, significantly impacts computation and communication. The integration of QKD with classical symmetric cryptographic algorithms in quantum communication technology is increasingly becoming a supportive force in the era of information.

4.1.1 The Foundation of Quantum Communication

In the mid-20th century, humans began to comprehend and utilize the laws of microscopic physics based on quantum mechanics, leading to groundbreaking technological advancements such as lasers, semiconductors, and atomic energy. In the 21st century, quantum technology has deeply merged with information technology, giving rise to the second "quantum revolution." One integral part of this revolution is "quantum communication," a novel communication method that utilizes quantum entanglement for information transfer.

We now know that quantum possesses extraordinary properties that classical physics does not exhibit, with quantum entanglement being one prominent feature. Before understanding quantum entanglement, a more familiar phenomenon is "telepathy." Simply put, it refers to two strangers, separated by a great distance, coincidentally thinking about the same thing, as if their minds are attuned to each other's presence.

Like "telepathy," quantum mechanics reveals that any particle in the universe has a "twin." Even if the entire cosmos separates these two particles, they remain in synchronized states, exhibiting identical changes. This synchronized state of two particles is called quantum entanglement. When two entangled particles are separated, no matter the distance, a mysterious correlation exists between them. Any change in one particle's state will immediately correspondingly change the other particle's state. In other words, we can infer the information about one particle by measuring the state of the other.

Another remarkable characteristic of quantum is its randomness in measurement and unclonable property—any measurement disrupts the quantum's original state. Regarding randomness in measurement, a photon can vibrate in a specific direction called polarization in quantum mechanics. Due to quantum superposition, a photon can simultaneously exist in a superposition state of horizontal and vertical polarization. When we measure this photon in two different directions, we discover that each measurement yields only one result: horizontal or vertical. The outcome of the measurement is entirely random.

Furthermore, in the macroscopic world, we can typically accurately determine an object's velocity and position simultaneously. For example, when measuring an airplane, radar can precisely determine its speed and position. However, measurement disrupts or changes the quantum state in the quantum world. If we accurately measure a quantum's position, its velocity becomes indeterminable. Since measuring a quantum's state results in random outcomes, people naturally cannot duplicate a quantum when it is unknown.

Under the randomness and unclonable properties of quantum measurements, it can be said that quantum communication, based on quantum characteristics, is almost impossible to decrypt. Traditional communication relies on complex mathematical algorithms for encryption, which can be cracked through computation. On the other hand, quantum communication ensures high security, being impervious to decryption and eavesdropping, which has been rigorously proven mathematically.

Furthermore, quantum communication guarantees security due to the properties of quantum entanglement, random measurements, and unclonability. In the process of QKD or quantum state transfer, if someone eavesdrops, the state will be altered due to the eavesdropping (measurement), resulting in a significant increase in the error rate of received passwords. This alerts both the sender and receiver, prompting them to cease transmission through that channel.

4.1.2 Secure Information Transmission

As a next-generation communication technology, quantum communication provides absolute security impervious to eavesdropping and computational decryption, lacking in traditional communication.

Secrecy and espionage have existed since ancient times, and there has always been an ongoing intellectual battle of escalating levels. The continuous development of modern secure communication technology aims to protect personal privacy and ensure the confidentiality of information between businesses and politics.

However, traditional encryption methods are always susceptible to decryption, especially with the advent of quantum computing, which can effortlessly crack many current encryption methods through parallel computation.

Specifically, in cryptography, the text that needs to be transmitted confidentially is called plaintext, while the transformed text through a specific method is called ciphertext. Transforming plaintext into ciphertext is called encryption, and the reverse process is called decryption. The rules used in encryption and decryption are known as keys. In modern communication, keys are generally based on computer algorithms.

In symmetric encryption techniques, the sender and receiver share the same key, and the decryption algorithm is the inverse of the encryption algorithm. This method is simple and technically mature, but it is difficult to ensure the secure transmission of information since the key needs to be transmitted through another channel. Once the key is intercepted, the content of the information is exposed. This led to the development of asymmetric encryption techniques.

In asymmetric encryption techniques, each individual generates a pair of keys, consisting of a public key and a private key, before receiving information. The public key is used for encryption, while the private key is used for decryption. The encryption algorithm is public, while the decryption algorithm remains confidential. Asymmetric encryption is asymmetrical in terms of encryption and decryption, as well as the sender and receiver. Therefore, it is known as asymmetric encryption technology. The public key can be easily derived from the private key algorithm, but obtaining the private key from the public key is extremely difficult. In other words, it is an algorithm that is easy to perform in one direction and extremely difficult to reverse. The widely used RSA cryptographic system serves this purpose.

The RSA algorithm, named after its inventors Ron Rivest, Adi Shamir, and Leonard Adleman, is based on a simple number theory fact: multiplying two prime numbers is relatively easy, but factoring their product back into the prime numbers is extremely difficult.

For example, calculating $17 \times 37 = 629$ is straightforward, but it becomes more challenging if given 629 and asked to find its factors. Furthermore, the difficulty gap between forward and reverse calculations increases significantly as the numbers grow. Breaking a high-bit RSA encryption with a classical computer is practically impossible. For a machine capable of performing 10^{12} operations per second, it would take 150,000 years to crack a 300-bit RSA encryption. However, using Shor's algorithm, this becomes effortless for a quantum computer, as it can break the 300-bit encryption in just one second.

Traditional encryption algorithms are becoming vulnerable with the emergence of quantum computers. Although the current most advanced quantum computers have only 70 qubits, the rapid development of quantum computing in the foreseeable future necessitates the development of more advanced encryption algorithms or using "provably secure" quantum communication.

Furthermore, as we have mentioned, quantum communication has the added benefit of being impervious to eavesdropping. The Prism Gate incident tested the security of global communication infrastructure, and in addition to robust encryption algorithms, preventing information from being intercepted is also a crucial factor in information security. In wireless communication, the radio spectrum is shared, and while encryption algorithms are vital, it is challenging to achieve one-to-one key distribution. For optical fiber communication, probing techniques can easily intercept light signals without detection by the communicating parties. In quantum communication, the indivisibility of single photons prevents eavesdroppers from obtaining the complete key. Additionally, due to the quantum uncertainty principle, once eavesdroppers perform measurements on the light signal, the quantum state of the photons is altered, causing a discrepancy in the key comparison between the communicating parties and leading to the detection of eavesdropping.

It can be said that in today's increasingly self-conscious data security landscape, quantum communication's development is becoming inevitable. The charm of quantum communication lies in its ability to surpass the limitations of existing classical information systems, providing a significant sense of security in the current lack of information security.

4.1.3 The Upgrading of Classic Communications

With quantum communication's development and progress, security measures are becoming increasingly complex and reliable. Humanity is committed to expanding quantum secure communication to longer distances and larger-scale wide-area networks.

For example, quantum communication holds significant potential and prospects in areas such as military, defense, and finance regarding information security. In the defense and military sectors, quantum communication can be applied to communication key generation and distribution systems, distributing quantum keys between any two users within the coverage area of future battlefields and establishing a secure military communication network. Quantum communication can be used for national-level confidential communication in military and defense and in government, telecommunications, securities, insurance, banking, industry and commerce, taxation, and finance sectors involving confidential data and documents.

In addition, quantum communication can also be applied to information warfare, improving the secrecy of military optical network information transmission and enhancing information protection and countermeasures. It can also be used for secure communication in deep-sea environments, opening up new avenues for secure communication in offshore and deep-sea settings. By utilizing quantum teleportation, absolute security of quantum communication, large channel capacity, high communication speed, long-distance transmission, and efficient information processing, a military information network that meets the special requirements of defense and military can be established, gaining an advantage in defense and military affairs.

Furthermore, in the national economy, quantum communication can be utilized for covert communication in financial institutions and monitoring and ensuring communication in important infrastructure such as power grids, gas pipelines, and water supply networks.

However, it is worth mentioning that quantum communication, despite its revolutionary power, is not intended to replace traditional communication. Quantum and classical communication are two different forms of communication, with quantum communication aiming to make traditional digital communication more secure.

In reality, QKD and teleportation rely on a "classical channel" that requires classical communication. In the case of QKD, the sender and receiver need to compare measurement methods through a classical channel and select the common part from the random measurement methods. Only the measurement results from this common part can be used as unconditionally secure quantum keys.

Similarly, in quantum teleportation, the sender and receiver must also compare measurement methods through a classical channel so that the receiver can perform the correct operations and accurately restore the transmitted quantum bits. Quantum teleportation utilizes quantum entanglement, and the classical channel prevents the transmission of quantum bits solely based on quantum entanglement. Thus, superluminal transmission of quantum entanglement beyond the speed of light, which would violate relativity, is impossible.

It can be said that quantum communication is a new battlefield beyond classical communication and a new development opportunity. For the communication industry, classical communication is like the chemical energy derived from coal combustion, while quantum communication is like electrical energy. Most electrical energy relies on chemical energy, just as quantum communication relies on classical communication.

Moreover, electrical energy will inherit and develop from chemical energy, allowing it to be applied in more areas to better control machines and process and transmit information. Similarly, quantum communication inherits and develops from classical communication. On the one hand, it enhances the security of classical communication, ensuring that information is not intercepted along the way. On the other hand, quantum bits can surpass the limitations of classical digital communication, making information transmission more efficient.

Ultimately, the charm of quantum communication lies in its ability to surpass the limits of existing classical information systems, providing a great sense of security in an era where information security is lacking. From theoretical advancement to practical application, quantum communication is upgrading the information age and triggering a technological revolution.

4.2 Applications of Quantum Communication

Quantum communication, as an important branch of quantum information science, utilizes quantum states as information carriers for communication. At present, typical applications of quantum communication include Quantum Key Distribution (QKD) and Quantum Teleportation (QT). QKD enables the secure transmission of classical information. QT is an effective means of transmitting quantum information and is expected to become the primary mode of information exchange in distributed quantum computing networks and other applications.

4.2.1 QKD

Simply put, QKD enables secure key sharing between the sender and receiver, ensuring secure communication through one-time encryption. Information eavesdropping can be prevented by leveraging the unpredictability and unclonability of quantum states. This process involves establishing a secure key-sharing mechanism between the sender and receiver, combining it with traditional secure communication techniques for classical information encryption, decryption, and secure transmission.

Since the proposal of the first QKD protocol, the "BB84," in 1984, QKD has gained significant momentum. The continuous research and development of its security aspects and the practical application of related technologies have proven the importance of QKD in combating quantum computing and constructing quantum communication networks.

Specifically, the first QKD protocol, the "BB84," was proposed in 1984 by American physicist Charles H. Bennett and Canadian cryptographer Gilles Brassard. The name "BB84" is derived from the initials of their surnames and the year of its proposal.

The "BB84" follows a two-party communication architecture involving a sender (Alice) and a measurement receiver (Bob). As shown in figure 4, Alice selects two sets of non-orthogonal basis vectors in the polarization dimension of a single photon. Each set consists of two orthogonal polarization states: H polarization and V polarization under the rectilinear basis and +45° polarization and –45° polarization under the diagonal basis. Based on classical binary bits (0 and 1), Alice encodes the light source into corresponding polarization states of single photons. H polarization and –45° polarization represent classical bit 0, and V polarization and +45° polarization represent classical bit 1. The encoded photons are then transmitted, while Bob randomly selects either the rectilinear or diagonal basis to measure and record the results.

After a certain period of experimentation, Alice and Bob publicly disclose the basic information they have chosen on an authenticated public channel. They then retain the information corresponding to the same selected basis to obtain a sifted key. Subsequently, they sample a portion of the sifted key to compare the consistency of information. If the error rate exceeds a certain threshold, the communication is deemed insecure, and the key generated during that communication is discarded. The process is repeated for subsequent communications until the results of the sifted key comparison meet the error rate requirement. Finally, data post-processing techniques such as error correction and privacy amplification enable Alice and Bob to share a segment of the same security key.

Due to the random selection of basis vectors by Alice and Bob during the key distribution process and the non-orthogonality of the two sets of basis vectors, an eavesdropper attempting to listen in would need to measure these unknown single quantum states. Due to the uncertainty principle, the measured quantum states would inevitably produce random measurement results, leading to an

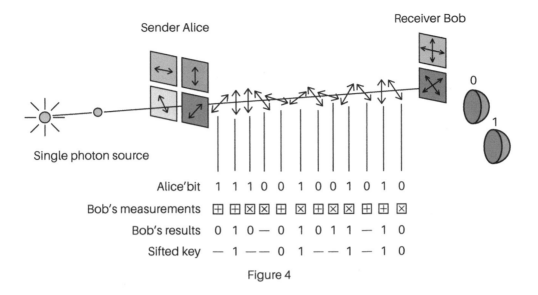

Figure 4

increased error rate in the sifted key comparison between Alice and Bob, thus detecting the presence of an eavesdropper. In addition to the "BB84," another QKD method is the "E91."

It is worth mentioning that in QKD, each bit of the key is transmitted using single photons. The quantum behavior of individual photons makes it impossible for an eavesdropper to intercept and replicate the state of the photons without detection. In contrast, in conventional optical communication, each pulse contains many photons, and the group's statistical behavior overshadows individual photons' quantum behavior. Therefore, intercepting a small number of photons from the massive flow of photons in optical communication cannot be noticed by the users at both ends of the communication, making the transmitted key insecure. The key aspect of QKD technology lies in generating, transmitting, and detecting single photon streams with various polarization states. Specialized polarization filters, single-photon detectors, and ultra-low-temperature environments make this technology possible.

However, in QKD, the transmission of single photon sequences in optical fiber networks results in data transmission speeds much lower than those of conventional optical fiber communication networks. It is not suitable for transmitting large amounts of data files and images but is specifically designed for transmitting keys used in symmetric cryptographic systems. Once the communicating parties have exchanged and confirmed the sharing of a secure key, this key is used to encrypt a large amount of data transmitted over an insecure high-speed network.

Although QKD has achieved significant research breakthroughs, it still faces several challenges.

The ideal scenario for QKD is to use statistical properties known as Bell inequalities to verify the security of the generated key solely through experimental tests without requiring trust in the devices used by both parties. However, to achieve such a level of security in practice, stringent requirements are imposed on the experimental devices. The imperfections of real world experimental devices introduce potential security vulnerabilities in the QKD system. Fortunately, after more than three decades of joint efforts by the global academic community, combining "device-independent QKD" protocols and quantum communication systems with accurately calibrated and autonomously controlled light sources can provide security under realistic conditions.

However, achieving higher code (key generation rates) and longer key transmission distances remains challenging in QKD. In terms of code rates, the team led by A. J. Shields at Toshiba Europe Research Laboratory achieved a code rate of 1.2 Mbps over 50 km in 2014. Regarding transmission distances, the team led by Pan Jianwei at the University of Science and Technology of China achieved QKD over a free-space distance of 1,200 km using the Micius quantum science experiment satellite in 2017. The team led by Hugo Zbinden at the University of Geneva achieved QKD over 421 km in optical fibers in 2018.

Nevertheless, the theoretical and experimental work on QKD mentioned above has yet to reach the limit of code rate distance for QKD without relays, where the receiving device does not produce any detection noise. Moreover, practical QKD systems mentioned above are further limited within the code rate distance limit because measurement devices inevitably introduce certain noise levels, reducing the code transmission rate. As the transmission distance gets longer and the channel attenuation gets larger, the signal count that the measurement device can measure gets smaller and smaller, and the noise generated by the measurement device takes up a larger and larger percentage of the signal, and when the noise percentage exceeds a certain threshold, the transmission process cannot generate a key.

4.2.2 The Application of QKD

Data Center Backup and Business Continuity

Quantum secure communication can be used to ensure the security of data transmission between different data centers for backup and business continuity purposes. Link encryption devices between data centers can replace keys on-demand through QKD to meet the high-security data transmission requirements of enterprises and users.

Government and Enterprise Network Protection

Quantum secure communication can be used to protect the security of government and enterprise network infrastructure and services. Enterprises or government agencies often require highly confidential, integrity, and authentic communication services and mandatorily adopt dedicated security systems. Secure virtual private network technologies based on IPSec or TLS are commonly used to authenticate and encrypt traffic between data centers and branch offices. QKD link encryption devices can be combined with these technologies to meet the information encryption requirements between various sites in enterprise networks.

Critical Infrastructure Control and Data Collection

Quantum secure communication can be used to protect the communication security of data collection and monitoring systems in critical infrastructure, such as Supervisory Control and Data Acquisition. Critical infrastructure plays a vital role in the normal operation of socioeconomic activities, and its security and reliability usually rely on the communication infrastructure subsystems. Information confidentiality, authenticity, and integrity are crucial in these communication subsystems. For example, signaling control systems in railways and water supply control systems can be protected by distributing keys through QKD.

Telecom Backbone Network Protection

QKD can be used to provide security services for communication between nodes in the telecom backbone network. The current telecom backbone network is often constructed using wavelength-division multiplexing (WDM) technology, providing multiple optical fiber channels. In addition to the channels used for existing services, reserved protection channels, and backup channels, additional channels are usually available. These spare wavelengths can establish QKD links, enabling high-security encryption of WDM business channels using quantum keys generated through QKD. For example, the quantum keys generated by QKD can be applied to encrypt the business data between OTN devices. The quantum, negotiation, and classical data channels carrying OTN services required by the QKD system can be transmitted through WDM. This technology has been verified as feasible through field trials.

Telecom Access Network Protection

QKD can be used in Passive Optical Networks (PON) in telecom access networks to ensure communication security. Through the QKD system, secure key distribution can be achieved between Optical Line Terminals (OLT) and Optical Network Units (ONU) in the PON network, enabling encrypted transmission of ONU user data and providing a new key distribution solution for telecom access networks. For example, the QKD system consists of an asymmetric tree-like network structure. Since quantum detectors are currently more expensive than quantum light sources, low-cost QKD transmitters can be deployed at each ONU, while a set of QKD receivers can be deployed at the OLT.

Long-Range Wireless Communication Protection

Combining QKD with wireless communication systems based on satellites, aircraft, and other flying vehicles is a promising application. It can achieve highly secure key distribution between remote sites without the need for deploying a large number of ground fibers and trusted relay stations. Satellites for exchanging keys through QKD can also be extended to scenarios with multiple satellites, connecting them through free-space links to form a global satellite QKD network. Compared to the atmospheric channel on the ground, the channel attenuation in space is significantly lower, allowing high-speed key distribution over long distances between satellites.

Mobile Terminal Quantum Security Service

Ensuring network security for various mobile terminal users has become a hot topic. By leveraging the unique advantages of QKD and combining them with a Key Distribution Center (KDC), the quantum keys generated by QKD can be applied to the mobile terminal side to protect the end-to-end and end-to-server communication security, which can be applied in various scenarios, such as mobile office, mobile operation, mobile payment and Internet of Things.

For example, the QKD network combines a quantum security service KDC for managing the quantum keys generated by the QKD network and a quantum key update terminal device near the user, which can charge the symmetric quantum keys generated by the QKD network to the secure storage media (e.g., SD card, SIM card, U shield, security chip, etc.) of the terminal for authentication and session encryption during its communication. This scheme ensures the forward security of the session key compared to the traditional KDC scheme. Moreover, the authentication and session key negotiation processes resist quantum computing attacks compared to the traditional public key infrastructure scheme.

4.2.3 QT

QT, also known as quantum long-distance transmission or quantum invisible transmission, is a new way of transmitting information. It utilizes the quantum entanglement effect to transmit the quantum information carried by quantum states. "Teleportation" refers to a "complete" form of information transfer detached from physical objects.

It is somewhat similar to the concept of instantaneously teleporting objects in science fiction movies. However, in QT, the information is instantaneously transferred, not physical objects. QT cannot transfer any tangible objects instantaneously; it can only "transfer" the information encoded in quantum states. By employing quantum entanglement, it becomes possible for a quantum state to mysteriously disappear in one place and instantaneously reappear in another. The term "instantaneously" here refers to the true physical meaning of being instantaneous without the need for time consumption.

From the perspective of the basic principles of QT, let's assume that the sender and receiver of the information are called Alice and Bob, respectively, and Eve represents a potential eavesdropper.

Now, Alice possesses a microscopic particle A, whose quantum state she herself does not know. She aims to transmit this unknown quantum state to Bob, located far away, without physically sending particle A itself. Achieving this is what we call QT.

To accomplish this goal, Alice and Bob must possess a pair of entangled "EPR" particle pairs. Let's assume that this entangled particle pair consists of E1 and E2. According to the principles of quantum mechanics, no matter which particle, E1 or E2, is measured, the other particle entangled with it will instantaneously undergo a corresponding change, regardless of the distance between them. Thus, the entangled particles E1 and E2 establish a quantum channel between Alice and Bob.

When Alice performs a specific random measurement on the entangled particle E1 and the particle A she possesses (measurement implies a certain kind of interaction), the state of E1 will change. At the same time, the entangled particle E2 held by Bob will instantaneously collapse into the corresponding quantum state.

According to the significance of entanglement, the state to which E2 collapses depends entirely on E1, which Alice's random measurement determines. Subsequently, the relevant information about Alice's measurement needs to be transmitted to Bob through a classical information channel. After receiving this information, Bob can perform a specific transformation on the entangled particle E2 (whose state has already changed), which allows particle E2 to be in the same state as the original quantum state of particle A (although this quantum state remains unknown). Once this transmission process is completed, A becomes invisible, and all its information is transferred to E2, hence the term "teleportation." Therefore, the entire process is referred to as "QT." Throughout this process, neither Alice nor Bob knows what quantum information they have transmitted.

It can be observed that classical information transmission methods are involved in QT, but this does not compromise the security of the entire information transmission system. The classical channel only needs to inform the receiver about the specific transformations performed by the sender and does not contain any information about the quantum state of particle A. Therefore, even if someone intercepts the information from the classical channel, it is useless.

This also means that QT cannot completely detach from classical behaviors; it still requires the combination of classical information transmission channels and EPR quantum channels to transmit quantum information. However, regardless, this represents a more advanced information transmission method than the classical one.

4.2.4 Access to the Quantum Information Network

Building quantum information networks has become a long-term goal in developing quantum communication, supported by QKD and QT technologies.

On the one hand, quantum information networks will rely on QT to transmit and network unknown quantum state information. The sender and receiver first prepare and distribute entangled photon pairs A and B, known as quantum entanglement distribution, to establish quantum communication channels. The sender then performs a joint measurement of the photon X containing the unknown quantum state information and the entangled photon A in a Bell state. The measurement results are communicated to the receiver through classical communication channels. Finally, the receiver performs a corresponding unitary transformation on the entangled photon B to obtain the quantum state information of the sender's photon X, completing the quantum communication process.

In this process, the physical carriers of quantum state information are single photons or entangled photon pairs, also known as "flying qubits." The transmission medium can be optical fibers or free-space channels. To overcome environmental noise, transmission decoherence, and channel losses, it is necessary to perform quantum state information storage and implement quantum relays based on quantum error correction, entanglement purification, and entanglement swapping. Various quantum state information processing nodes, such as quantum computers and quantum sensors, also require the conversion of matter qubits, such as electron spins and cold atoms, into quantum states of photons for transmission.

Quantum information networks achieve the transmission of quantum state information between processing systems and nodes using QT, enabling interconnection and communication among multiple quantum information processing modules. For quantum computing modules, due to the superposition properties of quantum states, interconnecting n-bit quantum state information can exponentially increase the representation space and the corresponding state evolution and processing capabilities by a factor of 2^n, expanding the capacity of quantum computing processing.

For quantum measurement modules, under the condition of globally entangled multi-parameter measurements, forming a quantum sensor network based on entanglement interconnections can enhance measurement precision and surpass the standard quantum limit, leading to applications in quantum clock synchronization networks and quantum-limited precision imaging device networks.

Furthermore, achieving long-distance end-to-end deterministic transmission of quantum states will provide solutions that are currently unattainable for enhancing secure communication capabilities and exploring new protocols for complex network configurations. Regarding potential applications in quantum information networks, preliminary progress has been made in domestic and international research and experimental verification. However, there is still a significant gap in practical implementation, with most efforts focusing on exploratory principles and conceptual experiments.

In 2012, the first measurement-based blind quantum computing experiment was reported by the University of Vienna in Austria. It achieved secure encrypted delegation of remote quantum computing tasks by placing the quantum processor in an entangled state and allowing a computational user to send unknown quantum states for controlled operations and retrieve the computation results.

In 2014, Imperial College London reported establishing interconnected channels between quantum computing units using a surface code error correction algorithm with a noise threshold of 13.3% and entanglement purification techniques. It achieved a computing processing interconnection frequency of 2 MHz but suffered 98% photon entanglement loss, resulting in a qubit interaction rate only in the kHz range.

In 2017, the Hebrew University of Jerusalem in Israel reported a quantum entanglement protocol algorithm based on multi-dimensional entangled cluster states for a multi-party leader election. It enabled leader election in cloud computing networks without requiring multi-party negotiations by utilizing pre-shared multi-dimensional entangled cluster states. By asynchronously measuring the shared entangled states, the measurement results determined the leader, ensuring randomness and fairness in the election process.

In 2020, the University of Science and Technology of China reported a quantum secure time synchronization experiment based on the "Micius" satellite and bidirectional free-space QKD technology. The satellite and ground station achieved single-photon level time synchronization signal transmission at a pulse frequency of 9 kHz. The quantum channel had an error rate of 1%, and the time transfer accuracy reached 30 ps. This experiment advanced the exploration of a satellite-based quantum time synchronization network.

As a comprehensive form integrating quantum state information transmission, conversion, relaying, and processing, quantum information networks represent a long-term goal in developing quantum communication technology. Based on the requirements of critical enabling technologies and expected application scenarios, the development and networking of quantum information networks can be roughly divided into three stages: quantum encryption networks, quantum storage networks, and quantum computing networks.

Quantum encryption networks can be considered the initial stage of quantum information networks. They utilize probabilistic preparation and measurement of quantum superposition or entangled states to achieve encryption functionalities such as key distribution, secure identification, and location verification. The typical application that has already reached practical implementation is QKD networks. In China's research and application exploration in quantum communication, the focus is currently on the level of quantum encryption networks. Due to the impracticality of quantum storage and relaying technology, long-distance QKD transmission and networking rely on the "trusted relays" scheme with key delivery in stages.

Quantum storage networks are the focus of research and application exploration in the next stage of quantum information networks. They will possess functionalities and capabilities such as deterministic entanglement distribution, quantum state storage, and entanglement relaying, supporting new applications like blind quantum computing, quantum time-frequency synchronization networking, and extension of quantum measurement baselines. Quantum storage networks are an essential direction of research and application exploration in future quantum communication, and foreign countries have begun discussions and efforts in fundamental components, system integration, network experiments, and protocol development. The development trends in this area should be closely monitored and valued.

Quantum computing networks represent an advanced stage of quantum information networks after integrating mature key technologies. They will incorporate functionalities and capabilities such as fault-tolerant and error-corrected universal quantum computing and large-scale quantum entanglement networking. Quantum computing networks can be used for distributed quantum computing to enhance quantum state information processing capabilities and to realize applications such as quantum entanglement protocol networking. It should be noted that, at the current stage, the potential applications and technological transformations that may arise in the ultimate form of quantum computing networks can only be glimpsed, and a comprehensive prediction and analysis are not yet conducted. Still, the possibilities and imagination therein may be equal to those of the Internet today.

4.3   Quantum Communication Worldwide

Quantum secure communication is a leading technology direction in quantum information that has entered practical implementation. Compared to traditional communication, quantum communication offers absolute security and is expected to be deployed first in fields with high requirements for information security. It is still in the pilot application stage, but with technological upgrades and cost reduction, quantum communication is poised to expand into the commercial sector with enormous market potential.

In recent years, countries worldwide have been gradually carrying out pilot applications of quantum communication. In the 1990s, the US was the first to include quantum technology in its national strategy. In 2003, Harvard University established the world's first experimental network for secure quantum communication in the US. The European Union (EU) also focused on supporting quantum communication research from the 5th Framework Program in the 1990s. Several countries then conducted QKD network verification through projects such as SECCOQC and SwissQuantum.

In the 21st century, countries like Japan, South Korea, and Singapore have begun to make efforts in this field. Japan classified quantum communication as a national high-tech development project in 2000 and formulated a ten-year long-term research plan. South Korea and other countries have also invested heavily in research resources, establishing quantum communication research centers and specialized institutions to make breakthroughs in this field. Although China started relatively late in quantum communication, with policy support and significant funding, we have achieved remarkable success and led the world in pilot application quantity and network construction scale. Our construction records are at the forefront globally.

4.3.1 The US

The US initiated research on quantum communication. At the end of the 20th century, the US government identified quantum information as a key supported topic in the "Maintaining National Competitiveness" program, with the National Institute of Standards and Technology (NIST) as one of the government agencies focusing on quantum information as one of its three key research directions. With government support, the industrialization of quantum communication in the US has also developed rapidly.

In 1989, IBM successfully conducted the world's first quantum information transmission experiment in the laboratory, achieving a transmission rate of 10 bps. Although the transmission distance was only 32 m, it marked the beginning of quantum communication experiments. In 2003, the DARPA of the US Department of Defense established the DARPA Quantum Communication Network between BBN Laboratories, Harvard University, and Boston University. It was the world's first quantum cryptographic communication network.

The network initially consisted of six QKD nodes, which later expanded to ten, achieving a maximum communication distance of 29 km. In 2006, Los Alamos National Laboratory achieved secure fiber optic quantum communication experiments with 107 km using the decoy-state scheme. In

2009, the US government's Information Science White Paper explicitly called for collaboration among research institutions to conduct quantum information technology research.

In 2009, the US government explicitly called for collaboration among research institutions to conduct quantum information technology research in its Information Science White Paper. The same year, the DARPA and Los Alamos National Laboratory in the US established multi-node metropolitan quantum communication networks separately.

In 2014, NASA officially proposed a plan to establish a long-distance fiber optic quantum communication backbone with ten backbone nodes, spanning a linear distance of approximately 600 km and a fiber optic skin length of about 1,000 km between its headquarters and the Jet Propulsion Laboratory. The plan also aimed to expand to space-to-ground quantum communication. In the same year, Battelle, the world's largest independent technology research and development organization, proposed a commercial wide-area quantum communication network plan. The plan aimed to build tens of thousands of kilometers of quantum communication backbone network around the US to provide quantum communication services for companies such as Google, IBM, Microsoft, and Amazon data centers. Los Alamos National Laboratory in the US is developing the next generation of the quantum Internet.

In April 2016, the National Science Foundation (NSF) listed "Quantum Leap—The Next Generation of Quantum Revolution" as one of the six major frontiers of scientific research. In August 2016, the NSF awarded US$12 million in funding to six interdisciplinary research teams to further advance the development of quantum secure communication technology. In September 2016, the NSF released the solicitation document for the 2017 Emerging Frontiers in Research and Innovation program, focusing on addressing fundamental engineering challenges, developing chip-scale devices and systems, and preparing for the practical realization of quantum storage and repeaters, with the goal of achieving scalable wide-area quantum communication and applications.

On July 22, 2016, the National Science and Technology Council (NSTC) of the US issued the report "Advancing Quantum Information Science: National Challenges and Opportunities," which mentioned that the US Army Research Laboratory (ARL) initiated a five-year multi-site, multi-node quantum communication network construction project to serve the strategic needs of the Department of Defense. On July 26, 2016, the White House issued an official blog post, recommending a strong push for the development of quantum information science and calling for prompt exchanges among academia, industry, and government on "quantum information science issues" to ensure the fulfillment of key requirements for quantum information research and development.

In June 2017, the National Photonics Initiative (NPI) in the US, a collaborative alliance of industry, academia, and government, jointly initiated a call for the "NQI."

In April 2018, the NPI released the "NQI Action Plan." The action plan encompasses four major areas: quantum computing for massive data analysis, quantum simulation for materials and molecular design, quantum secure communication, and quantum sensing and measurement.

In June 2018, the US House Committee on Science, Space, and Technology officially passed the "NQI Act." With the promotion of the NQI Act in February 2020, the US released the "Quantum Network Strategic Vision," focusing on the foundational development of the quantum Internet. In July of the same year, the "Quantum Internet National Blueprint" report was released, explicitly outlining the construction of a second Internet parallel to the existing Internet—the quantum Internet.

In September 2020, the US House of Representatives introduced the "Quantum Network Infrastructure Act," which called for the federal government to allocate US$100 million to the Department of Energy's Office of Science over the 2021–2025 fiscal year to advance the construction of national quantum network infrastructure and accelerate.

On January 19, 2021, the US NSTC issued the "Quantum Network Research Collaborative Pathways" report. Building upon the "US Quantum Network Strategic Vision," the report presented four technical and three programmatic recommendations for federal agencies to collectively take action to strengthen the US' knowledge base and preparedness in leveraging quantum networks.

In June 2021, Comm Star, a US-based company dedicated to encrypted quantum security products and services, announced the integration and operation of an advanced communication infrastructure for space data distribution. Within the Comm Star framework, Quantum Xchange would provide quantum secure encryption to ensure end-to-end protection of the entire lunar network.

Integrating services offered by their collaborative partners, global infrastructure, and comprehensive services would enable commercial, civilian scientific, and government entities to create, store, and transmit space data through a highly secure and quantum-protected network.

4.3.2 The EU

As early as the 1990s, Europe recognized the tremendous potential of quantum information processing and communication technologies and acknowledged their long-term application prospects. Starting from the EU's Fifth Framework Program (FP5), it has continuously supported quantum communication research across Europe and globally.

In 1997, a research group led by Nicolas Gisin at the University of Geneva in Switzerland achieved a plug-and-play QKD system. In 2002, a European research team conducted a QKD experiment over 23 km in free space.

In 2007, a joint team from Germany, Austria, the Netherlands, Singapore, and the UK achieved 144 km for decoy-state-based free-space QKD and entanglement-based QKD experiments between two islands in the Atlantic Ocean. The success of this experiment laid an important technological foundation for the eventual realization of inter-satellite quantum communication.

In 2008, the EU released the "Quantum Information Processing and Communication Strategy Report," which outlined Europe's quantum communication development goals for the next five and ten years. These goals included the establishment of ground-based quantum communication networks, satellite-based quantum communication, and kilometer-scale quantum communication networks integrating space and ground. In September of the same year, the EU published a commercial white paper on quantum cryptography, initiating standardization research on quantum communication technology and establishing the "Secure Communication based on Quantum Cryptography" (SECOQC) project, which brought together 41 partner groups from 12 EU countries.

This project was another large-scale international scientific collaboration following the European Organization for Nuclear Research (CERN) and the International Space Station. With a budget of €11.4 million, the SECOQC quantum communication network was established in Vienna, and cooperation with the European Telecommunications Standards Institute (ETSI) was initiated to promote the standardization of quantum-secured communication.

In 2012, physicists from the University of Vienna and the Austrian Academy of Sciences achieved QT over 143 km.

In 2016, the European Commission released the "Quantum Manifesto" with plans to launch the Quantum Flagship program in 2018. With a duration of ten years and a budget of €1 billion, the program aimed to maintain the EU's leading position in the quantum era.

On September 27, 2017, the EU published the final report of its Quantum Flagship program, which covered four major areas: quantum communication, quantum computing, quantum simulation, and quantum metrology and sensing. The report defined quantum communication as technologies based on quantum random number generators (QRNG) and QKD to achieve secure communication, long-term secure storage, cryptographic applications in cloud computing, and a "quantum Internet" for the distribution of entangled quantum states. The report outlined specific technological milestones to be achieved over ten years, as shown in the table below.

EU Quantum Flagship program technological milestones

Timeline	Goals
Within three years	The goals are to develop and certify QRNG and QKD devices and systems, research and develop new protocols and applications that meet the high-speed, high maturity (Technology Readiness Level, TRL), and low-cost deployment requirements of network operations. Additionally, systems and protocols for quantum relays, quantum memories, and long-distance quantum communication will be developed.
Within six years	The objectives are to develop cost-effective and scalable QKD devices and systems, deploy QKD networks for intercity and metropolitan areas, demonstrate end-to-end business applications for end-users. Simultaneously, research will be conducted on scalable quantum network solutions for various quantum devices and systems, including quantum sensors and quantum computing processors.
Within ten years	The aim is to develop an autonomous quantum metropolitan network based on long-distance (> 1,000 km) quantum entanglement, commonly referred to as the "Quantum Internet." Furthermore, corresponding protocols based on the new characteristics of quantum communication will be developed.

In 2019, supported by the Quantum Flagship program, Europe made significant efforts to build the Quantum Communication Infrastructure (QCI) with the aim of enhancing Europe's capabilities in network security and communication by establishing ground and space-based quantum communication facilities. In September 2019, the Open European Quantum Key Distribution (OPNEQKD) project was launched to conduct use case testing based on QCI in 12 European countries. Currently, QCI is supported under the Digital Europe Program.

On March 3, 2020, the Strategic Advisory Board of the Quantum Flagship Program officially submitted the "Strategic Work Plan for the Quantum Flagship Program" report to the European Commission, outlining the development of long-distance fiber optic quantum communication networks and satellite-based quantum communication networks to ultimately achieve a quantum Internet.

In June 2021, the European Commission announced the selection of a consortium of multiple companies and research institutions to study the design of the future European Quantum Communication Infrastructure (EuroQCI). EuroQCI will enable ultra-secure communication among the EU's critical infrastructures and governmental institutions. Led by Airbus, the European consortium, primarily composed of members from France and Italy, will integrate quantum technologies and systems into ground-based fiber optic communication networks, including a space-based component to ensure coverage across the entire EU and other continents. Ultimately, this will protect European encryption systems and critical infrastructure (such as governmental institutions, air traffic control, medical facilities, banks, and power grids) from current and future network threats.

4.3.3 China

China's achievements in quantum communication technology were made possible by the country's early planning and support. As early as 2013, China deployed the world's first long-distance quantum secure communication, "Beijing–Shanghai Trunk Line," taking the lead in the practical application and demonstration of related technologies and gaining valuable experience. In recent years, from the national level to local governments and departments, there has been significant attention and promotion of secure quantum communication to further maintain China's leading position in the industrialization of secure quantum communication.

In 2015, President Xi Jinping's "13th Five-Year Plan" proposal specifically emphasized deploying major scientific and technological projects that reflect the country's strategic intentions in areas such as quantum communication. The quantum information industry became strategically nurtured during the "13th Five-Year Plan." The development of the quantum communication industry as a national strategic industry has received support from various policies regarding national strategy, technological leadership, industrial promotion, and engineering construction. It is included in important national plans such as the "13th Five-Year Plan for National Economic and Social Development" and the "13th Five-Year Plan for the Development of National Strategic Emerging Industries." The National Development and Reform Commission (NDRC) also included the first-phase project of constructing a national backbone network for wide-area quantum secure communication in the list of projects to be supported under the New Generation Information Infrastructure Construction Project in 2018.

Various regional governments have directly supported the development of quantum technology and the construction of quantum secure communication networks through government documents. Provinces and cities, such as Anhui, Shandong, Beijing, Shanghai, Jiangsu, Zhejiang, Guangdong, and Xinjiang, included the development of quantum information technology and the construction of quantum communication networks in their 2018 government work reports and promoted their implementation. Particularly, the construction of quantum secure intercity trunk lines in the Yangtze River Delta region was included in the "13th Five-Year Plan."

In the "Outline of the Integrated Development Plan for the Yangtze River Delta Region" issued in 2019, quantum information also became a key industry in the future planning and layout of the Yangtze River Delta region. From the perspective of local policies, local governments in cities such as Guiyang, Haikou, Zaozhuang, Kunming, Guangzhou, Jinhua, and Nanjing, have also introduced relevant policies to support the construction of quantum communication networks. Following the release of the "Quantum Technology Innovation and Development Plan of Shandong Province (2018–2025)," the "Several Policy Measures of the People's Government of Jinan Municipality for Accelerating the Construction of the Quantum Information Mega-Science Center" was introduced as the first special policy for the domestic quantum information industry, laying a solid foundation for the local development of the quantum information industry.

China maintains a leading advantage in quantum communication, demonstrated in several aspects.

On August 16, 2016, China launched the world's first quantum science experimental satellite, "Micius," enabling the ability to conduct quantum science experiments on a space scale for the first time in human history. In 2017, it exceeded expectations by completing three major scientific tasks: satellite-to-ground absolute secure QKD, verifying space Bell inequality, and achieving ground-to-satellite QT. As a result, Pan Jianwei's research team from the University of Science and Technology of China (USTC) won the 2018 Breakthrough of the Year award.

Using the "Micius" quantum satellite, China successfully achieved thousand-kilometer-level bidirectional QKD, becoming the first to achieve QT from a satellite to the ground. This laid a solid scientific and technological foundation for China to continue leading the world in the development of quantum communication technology and at the forefront of research on fundamental issues in space-scale quantum physics.

In September 2017, China became the first country to complete the Beijing–Shanghai Trunk Line and opened the world's first quantum secure communication trunk line. At the same time, China was also the first to deploy a large-scale quantum secure communication network. After the Beijing–Shanghai Trunk Line was completed, it was connected to the "Micius" quantum science experimental satellite, forming the embryonic form of an integrated quantum communication network between space and ground. This marked China's entry into the wide-area network phase and officially ushered in a new era of industrialization for Chinese quantum communication.

Furthermore, China has achieved an independent supply of core components and is leading several core technological research areas. For example, in November 2016, collaboration among institutions such as the USTC, Tsinghua University, Shanghai Institute of Microsystem and Information Technology (SIMIT) of the Chinese Academy of Sciences, and Jinan Institute of Quantum Technology Research improved the secure transmission distance of secure quantum communication to 404 km. At 102 km, the secure code rate was sufficient to guarantee secure voice communication.

In September 2019, collaboration among the USTC, Tsinghua University, SIMIT, and other institutions successfully conducted dual-field QKD experiments in a 300 km real-world fiber environment, verifying the feasibility of long-distance QKD over 700 km of fiber. This marked an important milestone in practical dual-field QKD.

In March 2020, collaboration among the USTC, Tsinghua University, Jinan Institute of Quantum Technology Research, and other institutions achieved dual-QKD and phase-matching QKD over a 500 km real-world fiber environment with a transmission distance reaching 509 km.

In 2021, China continued to achieve multiple world-leading accomplishments.

First, China constructed the world's first integrated space-ground quantum communication network. Based on the secure quantum communication Beijing–Shanghai Trunk Line and the "Micius" quantum science experimental satellite, China built the world's first integrated space-ground wide-area quantum communication network in 2021. It achieved large-scale, multi-user QKD over a ground span of 4,600 km, demonstrating that wide-area quantum communication technology has reached a preliminary stage of practical application. Guodun Quantum provided the secure communication network's core quantum devices and technical support. On January 7, the research team published a paper titled "Integrated Space-Ground Quantum Communication Network spanning 4,600 km" in the international academic journal *Nature*, with Guodun Quantum as a major participating unit.

Second, China established a 500 km unrelayed fiber quantum communication network. In June 2021, a joint research team of the USTC, Jinan Institute of Quantum Technology Research, and Guodun Quantum broke through the distance limit of on-site long-distance high-performance single-photon interference technology using existing commercial fiber links. They used two technical schemes to achieve 500 km level dual-field QKD (TF-QKD), setting a new world record for on-site unrelayed fiber QKD transmission distance. Technical personnel from Guodun Quantum participated in the experiment and provided the QKD hardware platform and electronic control system.

The experiment employed two technical schemes to overcome technical challenges: laser injection locking was used to achieve 428 km TF-QKD, and time-frequency transfer technology was used to achieve 511 km TF-QKD. The research team developed laser injection locking and time-frequency transmission technology based on the SNS-TF-QKD ("send-not send" dual-field QKD) protocol. They locked the wavelengths of two independent lasers separated by hundreds of kilometers in the field to be the same. Additionally, they developed a real-time compensation system for fiber length and polarization variations in the complex field link environment. Furthermore, they carefully designed the wavelength of the QKD light source and filtered out crosstalk noise from other services in the field fiber cable using narrowband filtering. Finally, in combination with high-count-rate low-noise single-photon detectors developed by the SIMIT of the Chinese Academy of Sciences, they extended the secure coding distance of unrelayed fiber QKD to over 500 km.

Third, the fusion application of QKD and Post-Quantum Cryptography (PQC) was achieved. In May 2021, a joint research team from the USTC, Shanghai Jiao Tong University, Yunnan University, and companies such as Guodun Quantum and Guoke Quantum announced the first successful fusion application of QKD and PQC in the international community. The experimental equipment used QKD products developed by Guodun Quantum, and the Guodun Quantum research and development team designed the communication between the QKD equipment and the PQC host computer in the experiment. They built the experimental platform and completed data collection and analysis for QKD+PQC network experiments. All parties promoted the integrated development of quantum security technology by leveraging their scientific research and industrial advantages.

In August 2021, a joint team composed of Guodun Quantum, the USTC, Guoke Quantum, Jinan Institute of Quantum Technology Research, and Shanghai Jiao Tong University completed the world's first on-site verification of the fusion usability of QKD and PQC. The related work was published as an editor-recommended article in the prestigious academic journal *Optics Letters*. This research further validated the feasibility of the fusion solution in practical on-site operations. The team integrated the PQC authentication protocol into the QKD equipment and conducted long-term operational tests under multi-user and on-site communication conditions. In the experiment, researchers used

Guodun Quantum's QKD equipment with a system frequency of 40 MHz for protocol integration. The PQC authentication protocol participated in all QKD protocol data interaction stages, including basis reconciliation, error correction, secret enhancement, and key verification.

Fourthly, China achieved the first-ever 15-user quantum secure direct communication (QSDC) network. In September 2021, a team led by Chen Xianfeng from Shanghai Jiao Tong University, in collaboration with Li Yuanhua from Jiangxi Normal University and others, constructed a 15-user QSDC network. They utilized the principles of QSDC to achieve secure communication among 15 users in the network, with a transmission distance of up to 40 km. This achievement laid the foundation for future satellite-based and global quantum communication networks.

To enable the widespread application of QSDC, the researchers built a fully connected entanglement-based QSDC network consisting of 5 subnets and 15 users. The fidelity of the shared entangled states between any two users was above 97%. The results demonstrated that even when any two users performed QSDC over a 40 km optical fiber, the fidelity of their shared entangled states remained above 95%, and the information transmission rate remained above 1 Kbps, proving the feasibility of the proposed QSDC network. The network exhibited excellent scalability, where each user was interconnected with any other user through shared entangled photons of different wavelengths. Furthermore, by utilizing high-performance detectors and high-speed control of polarization modulators, the information transmission rate could be increased to over 100 Kbps.

Last, the USTC, Guodun Quantum, and others achieved a 46-node quantum metropolitan area network (QMAN). In October 2021, researchers including Pan Jianwei, Chen Tengyun, Peng Chengzhi, Zhao Yong from USTC, Ma Xiongfeng from Tsinghua University, and researchers from Guodun Quantum and Ningbo University presented the field operation of a 46-node QMAN in a paper published in *npj Quantum Information*.

Using standard network maintenance equipment with scalable configurations, the team operated the network continuously for 31 months, implementing different topological structures. They achieved QKD pairing and key management through a sophisticated key control center. The network supported practical applications, including real-time voice calls, SMS, file transfers, and one-time-pad encryption, enabling simultaneous audio conversations among 11 pairs of users. This technology can be integrated with intercity quantum backbone networks and form a global quantum network through ground-satellite links.

4.4   Challenges of Quantum Communication

As a powerful means to address the challenges of cryptographic security, the theoretical effectiveness and practical feasibility of quantum communication have been widely validated. Quantum communication schemes based on physical principles and cryptographic schemes based on computational complexity complement each other. They can effectively build a multi-layered defense for information security, enhancing the future capability of defending network spaces. However, quantum communication still faces various challenges before achieving robust network space security.

4.4.1 The Early Stage of Quantum Secure Communication

Quantum secure communication technology is still in its early stages of development and requires further coordinated advancements in technology, protocols, and applications to achieve large-scale industrialization.

First, regarding the underlying technology, the core of secure quantum communication is QKD technology, which manipulates and processes microphysical objects at a single quantum level. The technology obstacles to further breakthroughs in QKD capabilities include high-efficiency single-photon detection, high-precision physical signal processing, high signal-to-noise ratio information modulation, preservation, and extraction. Additionally, technologies such as optical/electro-optical integration, deep cooling integration, and high-speed and high-precision specialized integrated circuits are necessary to overcome the "thresholds" for miniaturization, high reliability, and low-cost development of quantum secure communication devices.

The breakthrough of these underlying technologies largely depends on research in new materials, new processes, new methods, and the support of micro-nano fabrication integration. They are characterized by great technical difficulty and uncertainty and face challenges such as high investment, high risks, international technological competition, and technological restrictions.

Second, in terms of industrial chain construction, as an emerging cutting-edge technology, the balanced support from academia, industry, and research institutions for forming and developing the quantum secure communication industry still needs to be improved. The industrial sector's involvement in research of the core underlying technologies of secure quantum communication is limited, with few companies mastering the core technologies for product research and development and limited supply capacity. Comprehensive and systematic solutions are lacking for products and applications, and joint research in application areas and infrastructure construction is just beginning. The industrial chain has apparent weak links. The construction and cultivation of these industrial chain links require coordinated efforts and accumulation in multiple directions, including the growth of the quantum secure communication industry's upstream and downstream workforce, integration with existing telecommunications networks, and enrichment of product systems.

Furthermore, quantum secure communication application scenarios are relatively limited, and industrial development relies heavily on government policy support. The subsequent commercial application models and market-oriented promotion and operation require further exploration. The involvement of the traditional communication and information security industry in the quantum secure communication industry is relatively low, making it difficult to establish and cultivate the industrial chain. The lack of demand-driven development motivation has resulted in sluggish progress in subsequent engineering construction.

Last, in terms of market ecosystem cultivation, on the one hand, from the user's perspective, quantum secure communication technology still carries a certain "mystique," and industries with security needs have a limited understanding of the methods and level of assurance provided by applying quantum secure communication. On the other hand, industry standards, qualifications, evaluations, certifications, and other systems are currently blank and require urgent development.

The quantum secure communication market ecosystem is still in a relatively fragile early stage. Like the early stages of developing industries such as computers and the Internet, secure quantum communication requires time to form market interactions through applications, promotion, certification, and regulation, thereby driving continuous industry upgrades.

4.4.2 The Standardization of Quantum Communication

The practical application and industrial-scale implementation of secure quantum communication still face numerous challenges. Standardization is a crucial aspect and plays a fundamental role in the future healthy development of the industry. Several domestic and international standardization organizations are engaged in QKD-related standardization work. These include the China Communications Standards Association (CCSA), the China Cryptographic Industry Standards Committee, the China Information Security Standards Committee, the International Organization for Standardization (ISO), the International Telecommunication Union (ITU), the ETSI, the Institute of Electrical and Electronics Engineers (IEEE), and the Cloud Security Alliance (CSA).

Quantum secure communication, an interdisciplinary and cross-domain system engineering, is still in the early stages of standardization. It requires collaboration and advancement among various fields and standardization organizations to quickly establish a comprehensive standard system supporting large-scale QKD networking, operations, applications, and certifications.

International standardization organizations are actively involved in standardizing secure quantum communication. Quantum communication is forming international standards, and relevant standardization organizations are accelerating their standardization efforts.

In November 2017, during the 55th meeting of ISO/IEC JTC 1/SC 27/WG 3 in Berlin, Germany, the China Information Security Evaluation Center, in collaboration with USTC Quantum Technology Co., Ltd., proposed the standard research project "Security Requirements, Testing, and Evaluation Methods for QKD" (Study Period). After multiple discussions, the project was successfully approved with the support of countries like Luxembourg and Russia. This was the first official international standard project in QKD.

In July 2018, during the ITU-T SG13 (Future Networks) meeting, South Korea proposed the standard project "Network Framework Supporting QKD," which was approved. In the same year, during the ITU-T SG17 (Security) meeting in September, South Korea further proposed the standard research on the "Security Framework for QKD Networks" and the "Security Framework for QRNG," both of which were successfully approved.

ETSI is a highly influential regional standardization organization in the global telecommunications field. In 2008, ETSI initiated the Quantum Key Distribution Industry Specification Group (ISG-QKD), which released six specifications over ten years, including QKD use cases, application interfaces, and transceiver characteristics. In 2019, ETSI accelerated its standardization work and published three specifications at the beginning of the year: QKD terminology, deployment parameters, and key delivery interfaces. They also initiated two new standards projects: QKD network architecture and security evaluation, resulting in 14 ongoing standardization projects.

In 2014, the CSA established the Quantum-Safe Security Working Group (QSS-WG), with USTC Quantum being one of the founding members. This working group has published several research reports, including quantum security definitions, QKD definitions, and quantum security terminology.

IEEE is an international professional standardization organization in electronic and electrical engineering. In 2016, General Electric (GE) initiated the P1913 Software-Defined Quantum Communication project in IEEE. The main objective of this project was to define a programmable network interface protocol for quantum communication devices. This protocol enables flexible reconfiguration of quantum communication devices to support various communication protocols and measurement techniques. The standard focuses on SDN-based QKD networks and designs protocols that specify quantum device invocation and configuration interface protocols. These interface protocols allow quantum protocols or applications to be dynamically created, modified, or removed.

In this context, China has also accelerated the construction of a standard system for quantum secure communication to promote the research and development of key quantum communication technologies, their application, and industrialization. In June 2017, CCSA established the 7th Special Task Group (ST7) for Quantum Communication and Information Technology. The goal of ST7 is to establish an independent intellectual property rights-based standard system for secure quantum communication in China. This system supports the construction and application of quantum secure communication networks and promotes international standardization progress in QKD.

ST7 consists of two sub-working groups: Quantum Communication Working Group (WG1) and Quantum Information Processing Working Group (WG2). The organization has gathered major domestic enterprises and research institutes in the quantum communication industry, with a current membership of 51 organizations. The specific goals of ST7's work include 1. Standardizing application-layer protocols and service interfaces to enable flexible integration of secure quantum communication with existing ICT applications, facilitating widespread adoption of secure quantum communication across various industries. 2. Standardizing network equipment, technical protocols, and device characteristics to build a deployable and scalable quantum secure communication network. This includes ensuring interoperability among different vendors' quantum secure communication devices, integrating QKD with traditional optical networks, and promoting the mature development of the quantum communication critical device supply chain. 3. Establishing a security testing and evaluation system for quantum secure communication systems, products, and core devices through rigorous security proofs, standardized security requirements, and evaluation methods.

ST7 has developed a complete framework for the quantum secure communication standard system. This framework includes standards for terminology, business and system categories, network technologies, generic quantum devices, quantum security, and quantum information processing. Within this framework, ST7 has initiated 25 standardization projects, including national standard projects such as "Quantum Communication Terminology and Definitions" and "Quantum Secure Communication Application Scenarios and Requirements," as well as industry-standard projects such as "QKD System Technical Requirements Part 1: QKD System based on BB84," "QKD System Testing Methods," "QKD System Application Interfaces," "Quantum Secure Communication Network Architecture," "Key Components and Modules for QKD based on BB84," and others. Additionally, there are 15 research projects underway, including "Research on Quantum Secure Communication Network Architecture," "Research on QKD Security," "Research on Quantum Secure Communication System Testing and Evaluation," "Research on Fiber

Transmission of QKD and Classical Optical Communication Systems," "Research on Continuous Variable Quantum Key Distribution Technology," and "Research on Software-Defined Quantum Key Distribution Network."

Five research projects have been completed, including Quantum Secure Communication Network Architecture and System Testing and Evaluation, QKD Security Research, and Fiber Transmission of QKD and Classical Optical Communication Systems. These projects have clarified QKD network architecture reference models, basic testing methods for quantum secure communication systems, security attack and defense techniques, and fiber transmission technologies for quantum and classical optical communication.

QUANTUM MEASUREMENT

5.1 Introduction

Mendeleev once said, "Without measurement, there is no science."

In addition to scientific pursuits, modern industry and defense have also placed increasingly precise demands on measurement. After all, the more precise the measurement, the more accurate the information it provides. The continuous improvement of measurement precision has accompanied the development of modern natural science and material civilization. Take time measurement as an example: from ancient sundials and water clocks to mechanical clocks in modern times, and then to quartz and atomic clocks in the present day. The precision of time measurement has continuously improved, enabling the continuous development of technologies such as communication and navigation.

Driven by the pursuit of higher precision measurement, in recent years, with the advancement of quantum technology and the advent of the second quantum revolution, precision instruments realized through quantum precision measurement techniques are pushing the limits of measurement precision for physical quantities like never before. Quantum precision measurement holds the potential to lead the transformation of a new generation of sensors, allowing us to measure matter with unprecedented accuracy.

5.1.1 The Transformation of Measurement

In the world of classical mechanics, that is, in non-quantum physics, "measurement" is defined as obtaining information about certain attributes of a physical system, whether material or immaterial. The acquired information includes velocity, position, energy, temperature, volume, and direction.

On the one hand, this definition of measurement may lead one to believe that every attribute of a physical system has a definite value, even a predetermined value, that is determined before the measurement takes place. On the other hand, this intuitive and natural definition may also lead people to believe that all attributes are measurable and that the obtained information faithfully reflects the measured attributes without exception, unaffected by measurement tools and measures.

In other words, in the world of classical mechanics, the state of an object can be measured, and the measurement process has negligible interference with the object being measured. However, after many centuries, this understanding of measurement was completely overturned with the advent of quantum mechanics and relativity in the early 20th century.

The revolutionary new theory of quantum mechanics disrupted everything in physics that was previously regarded as certain and unchanging: the nature of time and space, the concepts of simultaneity, identity, locality, and even the concept of reality with its strong intuitive appeal. Naturally, this also brought about a transformation in measurement.

According to the principles of quantum mechanics, observing or measuring a physical quantity at the quantum level results in random outcomes, and the object's state can suddenly change during the measurement. People can know and be certain of the probabilities of these outcomes occurring. This is similar to shaking a box filled with balls, like those used in lottery drawings, where each ball is shaken out randomly, and the probability of obtaining each ball is the same.

These probabilities are directly related to the wave aspect of the studied object. The "wave" refers to the wave proposed by Schrödinger based on de Broglie's research—every object, whether material or immaterial, has an associated wave. This mathematical wave, also known as the wave function, describes the quantum state. If we want to measure the position information, we can determine the probability of the object appearing in a particular location by knowing the intensity of the wave at that location through appropriate measurements.

Therefore, the wave function of a physical system can be seen as a special representation of a quantum state. This special representation depends on the positions of each component within the system (the position representation of the quantum state).

Quantum physics holds that any quantum state can be represented by certain special states known as eigenstates directly related to the measurement operations performed. The definition of these eigenstates for measurement is straightforward: all states that yield definite measurement results are eigenstates.

Furthermore, due to the collapse of the wave function, after the measurement, the measured physical system instantly collapses into an eigenstate corresponding to the measurement result. Therefore, after the measurement, the system's quantum state can be well determined and accurately known by people.

Moreover, from a quantum perspective, in fields such as quantum computing and quantum communication, the quantum state of a quantum system is highly susceptible to changes from the external environment, severely limiting the stability and robustness of quantum systems. Quantum measurement precisely utilizes this "flaw" of quantum systems, allowing the interaction between the quantum system and the physical quantity being measured to induce changes in the quantum state for measurement purposes.

Based on this, by manipulating and measuring the quantum state, and preparing, manipulating, measuring, and reading the quantum states of micro-particles such as atoms, ions, and photons, coupled with data processing and conversion, humanity will transition to a completely new stage in precision measurement. This will enable ultra-high precision and precise detection of physical quantities such as angular velocity, gravity fields, magnetic fields, and frequencies.

5.1.2 Three Technologies and Three Stages

It can be said that quantum measurement is a measurement technique that utilizes quantum properties to achieve higher performance than classical measurement systems. Consequently, quantum measurement exhibits two fundamental technological characteristics: first, manipulating and observing the target involves artificially engineered microscopic particle systems; second, the interaction between the system and the physical quantity being measured leads to changes in the quantum state.

From a specific procedure perspective, quantum measurement technology mainly includes key steps such as quantum state initialization, interaction with the physical quantity being measured, readout of the final quantum state, and result processing. According to the different applications of quantum properties, quantum measurement can be divided into three types of technologies: (1) measuring physical quantities using quantum energy levels characterized by discrete energy level structures; (2) measuring physical quantities using quantum coherence or interference evolution; (3) utilizing unique quantum properties such as quantum entanglement and squeezed states to further improve measurement precision or sensitivity.

These three types of quantum measurement technologies correspond to three evolutionary stages. Taking atomic clocks widely used in communication networks as an example, atomic clocks, which have been studied since the 1950s, use the hyperfine level transitions of atoms for time calibration, providing high-precision timing and network time synchronization for communication systems. However, atoms undergo intense thermal motion at room temperature, resulting in short coherence times. Collisions between atoms and the Doppler effect broaden the frequency spectrum, limiting the precision of time measurement. Therefore, cold atomic clocks began to employ laser cooling techniques to cool atom ensembles near absolute zero, suppressing atomic thermal motion. By using pump lasers for state selection and improving coherence time, the coherent superposition of atomic energy levels can further enhance time measurement precision.

In the future, it is possible to further explore the construction of a quantum clock network using entanglement between atoms to further reduce uncertainty and surpass classical limits. From discrete energy levels to coherent superposition and then to quantum entanglement, measurement precision continues to improve, but at the cost of increased system complexity, volume, and cost.

5.1.3 Five Technological Paths of Quantum Measurement

Currently, there are five major technological paths in quantum measurement, including cold atom coherent superposition, nuclear magnetic resonance (NMR) or paramagnetic resonance, spin-exchange relaxation-free (SERF) atomic spin-based measurement, measurement based on quantum entanglement or squeezing, and quantum-enhanced measurement techniques. By controlling and detecting the unique quantum properties of different quantum systems, precise measurements can be achieved in fields such as quantum positioning and navigation, quantum gravity measurement, quantum magnetic field measurement, quantum target recognition, and quantum time-frequency synchronization.

Regarding research and development trends in the five major technological paths, cold atom technology has gained momentum in recent years. Its advantages lie in reducing velocity-related frequency shifts, and slowed-down (or trapped) atoms can be observed for a long time, thereby improving measurement precision and potentially contributing to developing next-generation positioning, navigation, and timing technologies.

Furthermore, atomic spin-based quantum measurement can be classified into systems based on nuclear spin (NMR), electron spin (paramagnetic resonance), and coupling between alkali metal electron spin and inert gas nuclear spin (SERF). These quantum measurement systems are widely used in gyroscope and magnetic field measurements. They offer high precision, particularly SERF-based quantum measurement, which has a high theoretical precision limit and is another research hotspot.

In terms of the practical progress of the five major technological routes, quantum measurement technology based on quantum entanglement has the highest theoretical precision. It can surpass the limits of classical physics. However, its technological maturity is relatively low, limited by the preparation of quantum entanglement sources, long-distance distribution, quantum relays, and other technologies. It is mostly focused on theoretical verification or prototype development, and its prospects for practical application are uncertain.

Quantum measurement technology based on cold atoms has relatively high theoretical precision. Due to the existence of systems such as laser cooling and magneto-optical traps, it has a larger volume and higher cost. Currently, there are experimental studies on miniaturized cold atom measurement prototypes. Through MEMS technology, the measurement of electric, magnetic, and optical fields can be integrated, enabling chip-level manipulation of atom trapping, cooling, guiding, and splitting. However, the coherence time is relatively short.

For example, the US company Cold Quanta has provided commercial atomic chip products. In 2019, Huazhong University of Science and Technology reported a new type of subgravity MEMS chip with dimensions of 25 × 25 × 0.4 mm³. In 2020, the University of Birmingham in the UK reported an electro-optical chip based on dielectric metasurfaces for generating cold atoms with 599.4 × 599.4 μm² dimensions. Approximately 107 cold atoms were obtained based on the chip, and the cooling temperature needs to be as low as 35 μK. Still, the application conditions are demanding, mainly targeting high-end basic scientific research and other applications.

Quantum measurement technology based on the SERF principle has high precision. Research institutions are mainly focused on improving the measurement precision of magnetic fields and angular velocities. Enterprises have started to develop miniaturized SERF magnetometers and explore applications in magnetocardiography and magnetoencephalography. Although the precision of measurement based on NMR is not as high as that of cold atoms and SERF, the technology is relatively mature. There are already miniaturized and chip-based commercial products available.

Measurement techniques based on quantum-enhanced measurements result from integrating classical measurement and quantum technology. They utilize quantum technology to enhance the precision of classical measurements. These relatively mature techniques have broad application prospects in target recognition fields.

5.2 The Transformation of Sensors

As we know, quantum measurement enables precise measurement by manipulating microscopic particles such as photons, atoms, and ions and analyzing the changes in quantum states caused by the variations in the measured physical quantities. Quantum measurement not only allows a leap in measurement accuracy but also has the potential to lead the transformation of a new generation of sensors. After all, quantum precision measurement requires tools for practical implementation, and quantum sensors are the practical products of quantum measurement.

5.2.1 The Transformation of Clocks

The understanding and measurement of time is an ancient discipline. The concept of time and space unity can be seen in the ancient saying, "The four directions and up and down constitute the space, and the past and present form the time." The astronomical calendar based on celestial time has always been an important symbol of civilization. In the era of agrarian civilization, the accuracy of calendars significantly impacted social life. Sociologist Lewis Mumford stated in the modern industrial era, "The key machine of the modern industrial era is the clock, not the steam engine."

If clocks were the key machines of the industrial era, they remain crucial in the information age. Without modern clocks, the defining machine of the information age, the computer, would not exist. Clocks synchronize human actions and determine the speed at which computers perform billions of operations per second. In the information age, people have higher demands for the accuracy of clocks, and quantum measurement meets the new requirement for more precise time measurement.

Specifically, the accuracy of clocks comes from their time reference. For pendulum clocks, the pendulum serves as the time reference. Over 600 years ago, Galileo inadvertently discovered that the swinging time of a chandelier in a church was always similar for each back-and-forth swing. Based on Galileo's insight, Huygens became the person who created the first high-quality pendulum clock. In 1657, Huygens' clock represented a significant leap in timekeeping technology. Previously, the best clocks would deviate by approximately 15 minutes per day, while Huygens' clock had a daily error of only ten seconds.

However, even under ideal conditions where the only factors determining the swinging time are the length of the pendulum and the acceleration due to gravity on the Earth's surface, these minute differences can accumulate and affect the accuracy of pendulum clocks. Therefore, in the mid-19th century, people gradually developed increasingly precise mechanical timepieces based on pendulum clock mechanisms, achieving timekeeping accuracy that met people's basic daily timing needs.

Starting in the 1930s, with the invention of the crystal oscillator, compact and low-power quartz crystal clocks replaced mechanical clocks and were widely used in electronic timers and various timing fields. They have since become the primary timing devices used in people's daily lives.

Unlike pendulum clocks, the time reference for quartz clocks is a small quartz crystal. When a voltage is applied to the quartz crystal, it undergoes high-frequency physical vibrations. The frequency of the vibrations depends on various factors, including the type and shape of the crystal. However, the quartz crystal in a quartz electronic watch typically vibrates at a frequency of 32,768 hertz. Digital circuits count these vibrations, recording each passing second. Nevertheless, this level of precision is still insufficient for the rapidly advancing information age.

Modern electronic computers need to perform calculations within fractions of a millionth of a second, a billionth of a second, or even a billionth of a second. Modern technology requires a more accurate international standard time. For example, a quarter-mile deviation could occur for sailors navigating with a sextant if there is a one-second error. A difference of 1/1000th of a second could cause a spacecraft to deviate by 10 m. In each second, an electronic computer can perform 800,000 operations.

To meet the demand for precise time in the era of information technology, clock manufacturing shifted toward atomic clocks based on quantum physics and radio microwave technology starting from the 1940s. Atomic clocks became the most accurate clocks in the world. The electrons inside atoms emit electromagnetic waves when they undergo transitions, and the transition frequency is extremely stable. Atomic clocks, therefore, use these electromagnetic waves to control an electronic oscillator and regulate the clock's timing.

Specifically, certain atoms, such as cesium, have a resonance frequency. Electromagnetic radiation at this frequency causes the atom to vibrate or transition to a higher energy level. By stimulating cesium-133 isotopes with microwave radiation precisely at 9,192,631,770 hertz, resonance occurs. This radiation frequency is the time reference for atomic clocks, and cesium atoms act as calibrators to ensure the frequency is correct. Against this backdrop, in 1967, during the 13th General Conference on Weights and Measures, the definition of the second was revised: "The second is the duration of 9,192,631,770 cycles of radiation corresponding to the transition between the two hyperfine levels of the ground state of the cesium-133 atom." This marked the first significant contribution of quantum theory to the measurement problem.

Since then, the basic unit of time has permanently departed from the observable dynamics of planets and entered the realm of imperceptible behavior of individual elements. The accuracy of atomic clocks is almost unimaginable compared to Huygens' pendulum clock, which could have an error of ten seconds per day. If an atomic clock had started counting time from Earth's formation 4.5 billion years ago, its error today would be less than ten seconds.

The first atomic clock, the ammonia clock, was built by the National Bureau of Standards in the US in 1949, marking a new era in time measurement and timekeeping. In the following decades, atomic clock technology made significant advancements, leading to the development of rubidium clocks, cesium clocks, hydrogen clocks, and more. By 1992, atomic clocks were widely used worldwide.

The familiar BeiDou Navigation Satellite System currently utilizes atomic clocks for precise navigation. With the rapid development of quantum precision measurement technology, gyroscopes and inertial navigation systems based on quantum precision measurement offers advantages such as high precision, small size, and low cost. They will provide disruptive new technologies in seamless positioning and navigation. In this pursuit of higher precision in the technological race, atomic clocks developed by scientists from various countries continue to push the limits of science.

5.2.2 Quantum Positioning System

Currently, traditional mechanical and optical inertial navigation systems suffer from drift errors. Therefore, a new type of inertial device based on atomic interference technology has been proposed and extensively studied to meet the future demands for high-precision, fully autonomous, and reliable navigation across all regions.

Among them, based on the Sagnac effect, the atomic interferometric gyroscope measures the rotational angular velocity of the carrier. It is a novel inertial device that achieves high-precision angular rate measurement. Its inertial navigation function is typically realized in combination with an atomic accelerometer. For example, by using an accelerometer to measure the vehicle's acceleration and a gyroscope to measure its rotation, the motion speed and direction of the vehicle can be determined, thereby inferring its position.

Compared to traditional inertial measurement technologies, the new technology may reduce long-term errors and, in some cases, reduce reliance on sonar or geolocation systems. Furthermore, inertial navigation systems possess autonomy and are not constrained by time, space, or external environments, making them highly valuable in national security.

The development of atomic interferometric accelerometers is often accompanied by cold atom interferometric gyroscopes. The theoretical accuracy of quantum accelerometers is several orders of magnitude higher than that of traditional inertial devices. For example, in 2018, the UK developed a quantum accelerometer called the Quantum Positioning System (QPS). During submarine travel, the traditional inertial navigation system could accumulate a deviation distance of about 1 km a day, while the QPS only had a deviation distance of 1 m.

The principle of a cold atom interferometric accelerometer is similar to that of an atomic interferometric gravimeter. The former defines the direction of inertial measurement through the propagation direction of Raman light, while the latter measures atomic free-fall along the direction of gravity. Therefore, the performance of a cold atom interferometric accelerometer is comparable to that of a gravimeter. By transforming the Raman vector and spatially analyzing the atomic interference information, a multi-degree-of-freedom cold atom interferometric inertial measurement unit can be realized.

5.2.3 Gravity Measurement Based on Cold Atom Interferometry

Gravity sensors describe Earth's internal structure and crustal formations and assist in mineral resource exploration and navigation by measuring gravity acceleration and gravity gradients at different locations on Earth's surface.

Today, gravity sensors based on cold atom interferometry have become relatively mature. They are highly sensitive to the forces of mass interaction at extremely low temperatures, resulting in high measurement accuracy. The two most representative quantum gravity sensors are the atomic interferometric gravimeter used in geological exploration and the gravity gradiometer.

The quantum gravimeter based on atomic interferometry is currently the most maturely developed. It can be used with the gravity gradiometer for detecting underground structures, vehicle inspections, tunnel inspections, and Earth science research. It is expected to reduce costs in civil engineering and geological surveys and serve as a potential alternative method for fundamental physics applications. A few countries, such as the US and France, have already addressed the long-term stability and integration issues of cold atom interferometry systems. They are currently focusing on overcoming challenges in high dynamic range and miniaturization. The products are entering the practical application stage. China's Huazhong University of Science and Technology delivered a practical high-precision rubidium atom absolute gravimeter developed in 2021 to the Institute of Earthquake Research of the China Earthquake Administration. It is the first quantum gravimeter developed for industry sectors, marking China's entry into the top tier of international quantum gravimeter research.

The gravity gradiometer based on atomic interferometry exhibits high theoretical measurement sensitivity, low drift, and self-calibration capabilities. Additionally, it relies on all-solid-state devices at room temperature, offering engineering advantages and thus attracting widespread attention. It typically consists of two atomic interferometers operated simultaneously but separated by a certain distance. By comparing the gravity gradient measurements from the two interferometers and simultaneously performing differential measurements, it has the advantage of suppressing common-mode noise, such as ground vibration noise and Raman light phase noise. Gravity gradiometers are crucial in resource exploration, geophysics, inertial navigation, and fundamental physics research.

5.2.4 Quantum Sensing and Imaging

With the development of quantum information technology, quantum imaging has attracted widespread attention due to its enhanced detection sensitivity, imaging resolution surpassing the classical limits of traditional cameras, and advantages such as non-local imaging, single-pixel imaging, and lensless imaging. It has broad application prospects in high-resolution, incoherent, and imaging under harsh conditions and has been advancing toward practical implementation.

Quantum imaging utilizes photon correlations to suppress noise and improve the resolution of the imaged objects. Current technological approaches include Single Photon Avalanche Detectors arrays, quantum ghost imaging (coincidence imaging or two-photon imaging), sub-shot noise imaging, and quantum illumination. Potential quantum imaging applications include 3D quantum cameras, behind-the-corner cameras, low-light imaging, and quantum radar or lidar.

Taking quantum radar as an example, it holds promise as a new type of sensor for detecting stealth platforms. It has the potential to enrich the dimensions of target information, eliminate certain background noise, and outperform classical radar, thereby enabling the identification of stealth targets such as aircraft, missiles, and surface ships.

Stealth systems are particularly important for the military, so quantum radar has garnered significant attention from the US, Russian, and China military forces. However, quantum radar research is still in its early stages and has certain limitations. For instance, its detection range is not as extensive as that of traditional radar, and currently, it lacks operational value. The engineering development of quantum radar still faces significant challenges. Considering cost factors, it is expected to be deployed in specific regions to fulfill missions in the future.

Quantum radar can be classified into three categories based on the working modes of the transmitting and receiving ends: first, quantum transmissions with classical reception, such as single-photon radar; second, classical transmission with quantum reception, such as quantum laser radar; and third, quantum transmission with quantum reception, such as quantum interference radar and quantum illumination radar.

Research on quantum radar mainly revolves around three aspects: quantum entanglement interference, quantum illumination, and quantum coherent state reception. Notable examples of quantum radar research include the Quantum Sensor program and Quantum Laser Radar program initiated by the US DARPA in 2007. In 2018, China Electronics Technology Group Corporation showcased a quantum radar system at the China International Aviation and Aerospace Exhibition. In 2020, a research group from the Austrian Institute of Technology, the Massachusetts Institute of Technology, the University of York in the UK, and the University of Camerino in Italy demonstrated a quantum illumination detection technology using entangled microwave photons. Based on this technology, the quantum radar is less affected by background noise, has low-power consumption, and can detect distant targets without exposing itself. This technology holds potential applications in ultra-low-power biomedical imaging and secure scanning devices.

5.3 Quantum Measurements in Magnetic Fields

Magnetism is a fundamental physical property present in nature. From microscopic particles to celestial bodies, magnetic properties exist to varying degrees. Magnetic measurement technologies have evolved with technological advancements, ranging from ancient compasses to modern Gaussmeters and, more recently, superconducting quantum interference devices. These magnetic measurement tools have been applied in numerous fields, transforming human society. Quantum magnetometers have achieved significant breakthroughs by leveraging the principles of quantum mechanics.

5.3.1 Quantum Magnetometer

Quantum magnetometers, also known as quantum magnetometers or quantum magnetometers, are magnetic measurement instruments designed and manufactured based on modern quantum physics principles. Their distinctive feature is manipulating and controlling individual quantum entities such as atoms, ions, electrons, photons, and molecules, enabling measurement precision to surpass classical limits and reach the Heisenberg limit.

The macroscopic magnetism of objects arises from the magnetism of microscopic particles, primarily the magnetism of the electrons they contain. Through physical experiments, it has been discovered that many fundamental particles that constitute macroscopic objects, such as electrons, atomic nuclei, and atoms, interact with magnetic fields.

Quantum magnetometers hold the promise of improving sensor size, weight, cost, and sensitivity. Their physical realization has been developed in various quantum systems, including nuclear spin magnetometers, superconducting quantum interference device magnetometers, atomic magnetometers, and diamond nitrogen-vacancy (NV) center magnetometers.

Nuclear Precession Magnetometer

Nuclear precession magnetometer, used in geophysics applications, includes proton magnetometers, Overhauser effect proton magnetometers (OVM), and helium-3 (^{3}He) magnetometers. The first two utilize the spin magnetic moment of hydrogen nuclei, i.e., protons, precessing in an external magnetic field to measure the magnetic field. The ^{3}He magnetometer measures the magnetic field by utilizing the precession of the nuclear magnetic moment of ^{3}He in an external magnetic field.

Superconducting Quantum Interference Device Magnetometer

Superconducting quantum interference device (SQUID) magnetometers are magnetic flux sensors. This technology enables the creation of a macroscopic quantum system and allows for effective control through microwave signals. SQUIDs are one of the primary magnetic field sensors, but they require operation at low temperatures.

SQUIDs can be classified into low-temperature and high-temperature SQUIDs based on the superconducting materials used. They can also be categorized into direct current SQUIDs (DC-SQUIDs) and radiofrequency SQUIDs (RF-SQUIDs) based on the number of Josephson junctions inserted into the superconducting loop. DC-SQUIDs are made in a double-junction configuration with a DC bias, while RF-SQUIDs use an RF signal as the bias and employ a single-junction configuration. DC-SQUIDs can measure weak magnetic fields and are currently the most sensitive magnetometers, with sensitivities reaching 1 fT/Hz$^{1/2}$.

Atomic Magnetometer

Atomic magnetometers, or all-optical atomic magnetometers, encompass various technological paths. The main techniques to be discussed include optically pumped magnetometers (OPMs) based on optical-radiofrequency double resonance, SERF magnetometers for measuring low-frequency weak magnetic fields, nonlinear magneto-optical rotation magnetometers, and coherent population trapping magnetometers.

Diamond NV Center Magnetometers

Unlike alkali metal atomic magnetometers based on atomic vapor, diamond NV center magnetometers rely on solid-state materials and have garnered attention due to their high spatial resolution. The diamond NV center magnetometers principle involves coherently manipulating a single-electron spin qubit. The NV centers in diamond crystals, acting as electron spins representing quantum bits coupled with external magnetic fields. These magnetometers offer high sensitivity and biocompatibility without the need for cryogenic cooling. They find wide applications in the study of biomacromolecules and fundamental physics. Moreover, imaging biological signals using this material approaches the optical diffraction limit, providing excellent spatial resolution.

Magnetometric techniques based on single NV centers have achieved nanoscale resolution and sensitivity to measure single nuclear spins. In 2015, the research team led by Du Jiangfeng at the USTC used NV centers as quantum probes to obtain the world's first magnetic resonance spectrum of a single protein molecule under ambient atmospheric conditions. This study advanced magnetic resonance technology from billions of molecules to a single molecule. It provided a permissive experimental environment under ambient atmospheric conditions, making high-resolution nanoscale magnetic resonance imaging and diagnostics possible in life sciences.

In contrast to the magnetometric techniques based on single NV centers, those based on ensemble NV centers are typically aimed at measuring macroscopic magnetic fields. In applications, ensemble NV magnetometers have been used to measure magnetic signals generated by worm neurons, perform eddy current imaging, and detect minerals in paleomagnetic studies. China's research in ensemble NV magnetometry started relatively later, with teams from USTC and Beihang University conducting research in this field around 2016. In 2020, the research team led by Du Jiangfeng at USTC achieved a sensitivity of 0.2 pT/Hz1/2 in ensemble NV magnetometry by combining magnetic flux concentration methods.

5.3.2 Applications of Quantum Magnetometers

First, quantum magnetometers find extensive applications in biomedicine, including neurorehabilitation monitoring, brain science, cognitive neuroscience, brain-machine interfaces, precise diagnosis of cardiovascular and brain diseases, and in situ imaging of cells.

The main applications of biomagnetic fields are magnetoencephalography (MEG) and magnetocardiography (MCG) due to the relatively large neural conduction currents in the brain and heart, which generate strong surrounding magnetic signals. These non-invasive methods can positively impact the prognosis of patients and provide valuable information for clinical doctors to evaluate neurological disorders and surgical treatments.

The magnetic field strength of the brain is approximately 1 percent of that of the heart, making it more challenging to detect and susceptible to low-frequency interference. The detection of brain magnetic fields directly captures the magnetic fields generated by neuronal activity discharge, offering millisecond-level temporal resolution. It finds wide applications in diagnosing brain disorders such as epilepsy focus localization, brain functional localization, and preoperative planning. The popularity of magnetocardiography is expected to increase in the future.

Clinical studies on magnetocardiography in Europe and America have shown that traditional electrocardiographic examination methods can only capture 10% of the pathological information carried by cardiac electrophysiological signals, while magnetocardiography can complementarily capture the remaining 90% of cardiac pathological information. Magnetocardiography can reveal more extensive and profound cardiac pathological information than electrocardiography.

Fetal magnetocardiography (fMCG) is a novel alternative for antenatal monitoring, recording the magnetic field generated by the conduction currents in the fetal heart. Compared to fetal electrocardiography, the propagation of the magnetic field is relatively unaffected by surrounding tissues, giving fMCG the advantage of a higher signal-to-noise ratio. Additionally, it can be obtained in early pregnancy. The high temporal resolution of the signal allows for a more accurate determination of fetal heart rate parameters compared to fetal ultrasound.

Currently, the commonly used diagnostic methods for MEG and MCG in hospitals involve acquiring magnetic field data through SQUID magnetometers. However, the large footprint, complex equipment, high cost, requirement for liquid helium cooling, high operation and maintenance costs, and the issue of measurement accuracy due to the distance between the sensor and the scalp limit its widespread application. Moreover, the global helium supply is running low, necessitating the update and iteration of biomagnetic field measurements with atomic magnetometers to overcome reliance on helium cooling. The new generation of SERF magnetometers can achieve this goal. They are sensitive to low-frequency signals, operate at room temperature, have low-power consumption, are compact, and can be wearable. Their resolution is comparable to or surpasses that of SQUIDs, making them suitable for large-scale deployment. The shortage of helium has also driven related research and development.

In the future, quantum magnetometers can further explore biomagnetic fields. Brain magnetic field imaging, particularly in brain cognition, brain science, and brain-machine interfaces, is one of the few non-invasive functional imaging methods to achieve high temporal and spatial resolution. MEG serves as the foundation for brain imaging and human-machine interfaces. In the short term, a brain magnetograph may take the form of a helmet for continuous and remote medical monitoring and diagnostics in injury cases. It may be further developed to achieve practical, non-invasive cognition and communication with machines and autonomous systems.

Next, in industrial testing, the applications of quantum magnetometers mainly include metal detection, material analysis, non-destructive testing, and battery defect detection.

The main characteristic of quantum magnetometers is their ability to non-destructively identify the magnetic properties of objects or materials, thus controlling the quality of materials. This type of testing does not alter the tested material's characteristics, especially in metallic materials. When there are defects within the metal material, the conductivity of the material changes at the defect site. When alternating current is applied, a magnetic field gradient is generated at the defect site due to the principle of electromagnetic induction.

By measuring the magnetic field gradient, the location and extent of the defect can be determined. Currently, potential applications of non-destructive testing have been discovered in multiple industrial fields. For example, there is a market need for a fast and sensitive diagnostic tool to identify battery defects, assisting solid-state battery technology in providing flexible energy storage in a safe and efficient manner. As the popularity of new energy vehicles increases, manufacturers require a precise detection solution to reflect internal structural defects in lithium-ion batteries. Ensuring the safety of people's lives and property is of utmost importance, making it a major research and development direction for quantum magnetometers.

This technology requires extremely high sensitivity, and the main solutions currently employed are based on SQUID magnetometry and atomic magnetometers. Among them, atomic magnetometers offer advantages such as low cost, portability, and the possibility of implementing battery quality control and characterization techniques. The figure below shows a perspective of a diagnostic tool (sensor) that uses atomic magnetometry to measure the magnetic field around miniature solid-state batteries. It can provide information about battery manufacturing defects, charge states, and impurities and offer important insights into aging.

The UK's Center for Process Innovation has begun research on applying quantum sensors in industrial testing. The project duration is from August 2020 to August 2023, with £5.4 million funding provided by Innovate UK. The quantum sensor project aims to develop a pilot-scale system that can perform continuous online testing of batteries using OPMs. The system will have a series of OPMs as quantum sensors to detect the small magnetic fields emitted by qualified lithium-ion batteries. This technology can monitor the quality of batteries on the production line, quickly remove faulty batteries, and provide detailed quality assurance. The project will involve the development of the UK's manufacturing optical processing material supply chain, including steam battery production, laser manufacturing, optical packaging, magnetic shielding, electronic control, and data processing systems. The ultimate goal of the project is to create a pilot-scale battery testing system that can be implemented on a trial production line.

Third, in physics research, quantum magnetometers can assist in geophysical scientific research, geological exploration, and satellite magnetic surveys.

Earth has a strong magnetic field, which causes many rocks and minerals to exhibit weak magnetism or induced magnetization, resulting in disturbances in the geomagnetic field known as "magnetic anomalies." Artificial objects containing iron or steel are also often highly magnetized and can cause magnetic anomalies reaching thousands of nanoteslas in localized areas. Quantum magnetometers precisely capture the subtle changes in the geomagnetic field and obtain geomagnetic anomalies through geomagnetic observations. With the ability to accurately measure various geomagnetic samples, they can be used to study different types of geomagnetic samples from the ocean, lakes, loess, and other sources. They have broad scientific research and market potential in fundamental physics research, environmental and climate change studies, geodynamic processes, tectonics and magnetic stratigraphy, and deep-space and deep-earth magnetic field measurements. They can also be applied to drilling orientation in the petroleum industry, mineral resource exploration, and geological hazard early warning.

Furthermore, quantum magnetometers serve as powerful scientific research tools for studying the magnetic properties of materials and find wide applications in fields such as magnetic domain imaging, two-dimensional materials, topological magnetic structures, superconducting magnetism, and cell imaging. For example, diamond NV center magnetometers can quantitatively and non-destructively image magnetic properties by manipulating and reading the spins, enabling research on individual cells, proteins, DNA, single molecule recognition, and single NMR.

In geological exploration, quantum magnetometers are one of the most effective methods in geophysical exploration. They are widely used in various stages of geological exploration, including the search for iron ore and other minerals (including hydrocarbons), geological mapping, and structural studies. High-precision magnetic measurements also play an important role in archaeological surveys and engineering measurements. The systematic use of magnetometers for exploration dates back to the early 20th century. Over the years, at least four types of magnetometers have been used. In the first stage, optical-mechanical balance magnetometers were used for over 50 years. Subsequently, fluxgate, proton, and OPM were developed. Nuclear precession (proton) magnetometers and OPM are primarily used in magnetic exploration. Specialized magnetometers for ground, underground, marine, and airborne operations are widely produced to accommodate various measurement conditions.

In addition, quantum magnetometers can also be applied to space magnetic surveying and detection. Magnetometers used on satellites require low-power consumption, stable performance, and long working time, and some quantum magnetometers precisely meet these requirements. The spacecraft Cassini-Huygens, which explored Saturn and its largest moon Titan, was equipped with a helium optically pumped magnetometer to measure Saturn's magnetic field. The magnetic survey satellite SAC-C launched by Argentina was equipped with a fluxgate magnetometer (FGM) manufactured in Denmark and a helium-4 optically pumped magnetometer manufactured in the US. It was launched on November 18, 2000, with a lifespan of four years. Denmark's Oersted magnetic survey satellite and Germany's CHAMP dual-use satellite for gravity and magnetic measurements both utilized Overhauser magnetometers (OVM) to measure the scalar of the geomagnetic field, designed and manufactured by LETI (Laboratory for Electronics and Information Technology) in France. The European Space Agency is planning to launch the AMPERE satellite, which is also prepared to use OVM to measure the scalar of Earth's magnetic field.

Finally, high-precision magnetic field measurements are fundamental to geomagnetic navigation and anti-submarine warfare in the military domain. The military applications of quantum magnetometers mainly include military brain mapping for combat helmets, quantum navigation, anti-submarine warfare, underwater target identification, and seabed mapping.

Taking anti-submarine warfare as an example, quantum magnetometers can detect, identify, and classify target submarines and detect underwater mines, thus enhancing existing underwater detection capabilities. Magnetic field measurements are crucial for anti-submarine warfare because the magnetic alloys in submarines generate magnetic anomalies in the environment. Researchers expect that SQUID magnetometers can detect submarines up to 6 km away, while conventional magnetic anomaly detectors typically installed on helicopters or airplanes have a detection range of only a few hundred meters. Currently, quantum magnetometers are mainly used in airborne anti-submarine operations.

For example, CTF Corporation has developed airborne submarine detection instruments commissioned by the Canadian Department of National Defense. Public information shows that US military researchers require enabling technologies to enhance the performance of atomic vapor for electric field sensing, which can be applied in applications ranging from airborne electronic warfare to naval anti-submarine warfare. The US DARPA has signed a contract with ColdQuanta for the Atomic Vapor Science and Technology (SAVaNT) program, which spans four years. Among all the devices, vapor magnetometers have the highest scalar magnetic field sensitivity, focusing on achieving vector magnetic field measurements based on vapor in a small package.

Quantum measurements, as the future development and evolution of sensing and measurement technologies, have gained wide recognition in fields such as time standards, inertial measurements, gravity measurements, magnetic field measurements, and target identification. They have demonstrated tremendous potential in terms of market size and industrial prospects.

5.4   Prospects for Quantum Measurement

5.4.1 Quantum Sensors in Markets

Today, sensors are gradually being "quantized," and the long-term trend of quantum measurement is to quickly push quantum sensors to markets.

On the one hand, current classical sensors used in smartphones, cars, airplanes, and spacecraft primarily rely on electrical, magnetic, resistive, or capacitive effects. Although they are precise, they theoretically have limitations. Quantum sensors, on the other hand, have the potential to enhance sensitivity, accuracy, stability, and other aspects. Furthermore, certain applications require sensors that are insensitive to electromagnetic scattering. Quantum sensors can replace some traditional sensor markets and meet emerging specialized needs. The transition from traditional technology sensors to quantum sensors is an inevitable development trend.

Currently, some sensors have already been "quantized." For example, commercial atomic clocks have been developed in time measurement, realizing the "quantization" of time sensors. In gravity measurement, commercial atomic gravimeters have achieved the "quantization" of gravity sensors. Additionally, technologies such as "quantized" magnetometers and inertial sensor config-urations, including gyroscopes, accelerometers, and inertial measurement units, are undergoing verification for quantum sensor applications, and some prototypes of these products already exist. In the future, inertial sensors will play a significant role in military and commercial applications, enabling precise navigation without relying on external signals.

Overall, the main application directions for quantum measurement products and technologies include defense and military applications such as precision guidance and radar; space exploration such as timing and positioning; aerospace industry for aircraft navigation and positioning; metrology and scientific research; biological detection, medical diagnosis, Earth observation, geological exploration, engineering construction, and agricultural cultivation.

For example, in March 2022, the Royal Navy of the UK used quantum technology for the first time in a military exercise. They installed the MINAC (Miniaturized Atomic Clock) system developed by Teledyne e2v on the HMS Prince of Wales aircraft carrier. The MINAC system, which is the size of a laptop, provided time synchronization for the complex combat systems of the ship when the global positioning system failed.

In the development of autonomous driving technology, installing quantum sensors in cars can help accurately measure rotation, acceleration, and gravity during vehicle operation. Similarly, installing corresponding quantum sensors on ships, trains, and airplanes can improve autonomous driving functionality, enhance safety, and expedite the market deployment of autonomous driving technology. Additionally, the widespread application of autonomous driving technology relies on more precise, compact, lightweight, and consumer-grade quantum precision measurement products. Currently, most quantum sensors have relatively large sizes and cannot meet the requirements for mobile use.

In life sciences, there is a higher pursuit and demand for exploring the microscale, which has driven the development of advanced microscopy technologies. Additionally, in disease treatment, brain disorders, and heart diseases are common areas where treatment technologies still need improvement. The feasibility of next-generation brain and heart magnetography has already been demonstrated in experimental demonstrations. If further improvements can be made in miniaturization, wearability, and cost reduction, such technologies are expected to gradually become commercialized.

In communication development, the current mainstream communication standards are 4G and 5G, while 6G technology is underway. With the advancement of communication technology, there is an increasing demand for higher clock synchronization accuracy in communication networks, especially with many base stations. There is a greater need for compact, relatively low-cost precision timing devices to enable practical large-scale deployment.

Investments in GPS and magnetic resonance imaging (MRI) have already shown significant return value. Currently, there are many quantum sensors in different stages of development, and countries are coordinating efforts to shorten the time it takes to bring products to market and accelerate technology transfer. They are also continuously strengthening their leadership positions in their respective fields. Miniaturization, compactness, and cost reduction are the key objectives of major upstream suppliers while minimizing the impact on performance.

Cold atom technology, NV centers, and OPM+MEG (OPM combined with magnetoencephalography) are the technologies that hold the most promising prospects for commercialized quantum sensors in recent years. These technologies may find applications in various industries and scenarios. For example, SQUIDs offer higher sensitivity but require low-temperature environments, resulting in higher costs and stricter environmental requirements. On the other hand, OPM and NV center technologies can be used at room temperature, although their precision may not match that of SQUIDs.

From a global perspective, prototype products have been reported in various fields, such as quantum clocks, quantum magnetometers, quantum radar, quantum gravimeters, quantum gyroscopes, and quantum accelerometers. According to statistical analysis by BCC Research, the revenue of the global quantum measurement market increased from US$140 million in 2018 to US$160 million in 2019, with a projected compound annual growth rate of around 13% in the next five years. Research and Markets state that future 6G wireless technology will drive substantial progress in sensing, imaging, and positioning. Higher frequencies will enable faster sampling rates and higher accuracy down to the centimeter level.

According to ICV's predictions, the global quantum precision measurement market was approximately US$950 million in 2022, and it is expected to grow to US$1.348 billion by 2029, with a compound annual growth rate of about 5.1% during 2022–2029. In 2022, the quantum clock market held the largest share at around US$440 million (46.3%), with a compound annual growth rate of approximately 4.9% (2022–2029). Quantum magnetic measurement followed with a market share of around US$250 million and a compound annual growth rate of about 6.2% (2022–2029). Quantum research and industrial instruments held a market share of approximately US$200 million, with a compound annual growth rate of around 4.4% (2022–2029). Last, quantum gravity measurement had a market share of around US$60 million, with a compound annual growth rate of about 5.4% (2022–2029).

Currently, significant suppliers in the global market are concentrated in North America (primarily the US) with a share of approximately 47%. It is followed by Europe (mainly Western European countries and Russia), accounting for about 28%; then Asia Pacific (Japan, South Korea, China, Australia, and Singapore), accounting for about 21%. The US and Western European countries are the main technology exporters and buyers. In addition, the above-mentioned countries in the Asia Pacific are also the main technology buyers. Since most of the products and technologies in quantum precision measurement are developed and procured by economically developed countries, the remaining countries and regional markets account for a relatively small share.

5.4.2 Standardization of Quantum Measurement

Before quantum sensors can be brought to the market, there is a need to address the issue of standardization in quantum measurement. Research on standardization in quantum measurement primarily focuses on terminology definitions, application patterns, and technological advancements in the early exploratory stage. The standardization system has not yet been established, and the level of enterprise participation is relatively low.

It is important to note that quantum measurement encompasses various technological directions and application areas, which results in significant differences in terminology definitions, performance metrics, and testing methods. Therefore, standardization research is necessary for application development, test validation, and industry advancement.

It is crucial to conduct standardization research on overall technical requirements, evaluation systems, testing methods, and component interfaces for technologies that have already reached the prototype or preliminary practical stage. Multiple international and China standardization organizations are conducting preliminary standardization research and exploration in quantum measurement.

In 2018, the Internet Engineering Task Force initiated the Quantum Internet Research Group, which studies quantum Internet application cases. Currently, it includes two use cases: quantum clock networks and entangled quantum sensing networks for microwave frequency measurement.

In 2019, ITU-T established the Focus Group on Quantum Information Technology for Networks (FG-QIT4N) to research quantum information technology from the perspectives of terminology definitions, application cases, network impact, and maturity. Twelve manuscripts on quantum time-frequency synchronization were submitted and accepted for inclusion in the research report. CCSA-ST7 initiated a research project in the Quantum Information Processing Working Group (WG2) titled "Evolution of Quantum Time Synchronization Technology and Its Application in Communication Networks" to conduct research on quantum time synchronization technology.

In 2020, TC578 initiated a research project titled "Research on Testing Standards for Ultra-High-Sensitivity Atomic Inertial Measurement" to study measurement and testing methods for quantum inertial measurement.

For China, standardization research in quantum measurement should focus on the following aspects. First, lay out the construction of a standardization system and accelerate standardization work in areas such as overall technical requirements, key terminology definitions, performance evaluation systems, and scientific testing methods. Second, leverage the role of enterprises in standard development, support the establishment of key domain standard promotion alliances or focus groups, and coordinate product development with standardization efforts. Third, encourage and support enterprises, research institutes, industry organizations, and others to participate in international standardization discussions to enhance the involvement of Chinese research institutions and industrial companies in international standard research.

In summary, the quantum measurement industry is still in the early stages of development. It requires collaborative efforts from various stakeholders to promote technological advancements, industry adoption, and the realization of research outcomes and commercialization.

5.5 Research on Quantum Measurement

Currently, research related to quantum precision measurement has been carried out in many countries and regions worldwide. The main research areas include improving measurement performance indicators, further challenging measurement precision records, and surpassing classical measurement limits. Progress has been made in advancing prototype system engineering and conducting research on miniaturization, chip integration, and mobility to enhance system practicality. However, compared to foreign research, there is still a particular gap in progress within China.

5.5.1 Breakthroughs in Quantum Measurement

In recent years, domestic and international research in various fields of quantum measurement has achieved sustained breakthroughs in high precision and engineering aspects. Representative achievements include the following: In 2019, the NIST in the US reported an uncertainty indicator for an Al+ ion optical clock at the 10^{-19} level, further breaking the world record. In 2019, the USTC reported the realization of a high-precision multifunctional quantum probe based on diamond NV centers with a spatial resolution of 50 nm. In 2019, the University of California, Berkeley reported the development of a portable high-sensitivity atomic interferometric gravity sensor and a millimeter-level atomic nucleus magnetic resonance gyroscope chip.

Regarding the development of high-performance prototype indicators in specific areas of quantum measurement, the National Institute of Metrology (NIM) in China has developed. It is optimizing the NIM6 cesium fountain clock, which is at a similar level to the world's advanced standards. The USTC reported in the journal *Science* the use of diamond NV centers as protein magnetic resonance probes, achieving the detection of the magnetic resonance spectrum of individual protein molecules for the first time. In 2020, a joint team from Beihang University, East China Normal University, and Shanxi University completed the development of a super-sensitive inertial measurement platform and a magnetic field measurement platform based on the atomic SERF effect. The sensitivity indicators reached the advanced international level.

Regarding data post-processing for quantum measurement, introducing AI algorithms to enhance processing capabilities is becoming an emerging research direction. Quantum measurement uses atomic or photonic carriers as measurement "probes," and their signal strength is weak, making them susceptible to noise interference. For example, in conventional NMR systems, coherence time, magnetic noise, controller noise, and diffusion-induced noise are negligible. However, for diamond NV center nanoscale NMR probes, noise has a significant impact, and the noise model is complex, making it difficult to compensate or suppress through signal processing. Achieving the desired signal-to-noise ratio requires complex noise-shielding devices and precise control systems.

Similarly, in coherent measurement systems based on atoms, the thermal motion and mutual collisions of atoms cause spectral line broadening, resulting in decreased measurement precision. It is necessary to introduce techniques such as laser cooling and magneto-optical traps to prepare cold atoms, reduce noise interference, and obtain high signal-to-noise ratios. Introducing complex control systems or shielding devices is not conducive to the miniaturization and practicality of measurement systems.

AI algorithms are suitable for solving math problems with complex models and unknown parameters. They do not require prior knowledge of the mathematical noise model and can iteratively learn to seek answers or approximate solutions. By combining quantum measurement with AI technology, data post-processing capabilities can be improved, effectively reducing noise suppression requirements, simplifying system design, and enhancing practicality.

In 2019, the University of Bristol in the UK introduced machine learning algorithms for data processing in diamond NV center magnetometers, achieving similar measurement precision without needing low-temperature conditions and enhancing the practicality of single-spin quantum sensors. In 2019, the Hebrew University of Jerusalem in Israel reported enhancing the performance of diamond NV center nanoscale NMR systems through deep learning algorithms. In 2020, MIT in the US reported a generalized approach using machine learning algorithms to enhance the readout performance of quantum states.

Combining quantum measurement techniques with classical measurement techniques can also improve the performance indicators of quantum measurement systems. Quantum measurement systems based on cold atoms have the advantage of high measurement precision but limited dynamic range, while traditional classical measurement techniques have a larger measurement range. Combining the two can complement each other's strengths.

In 2018, the French Aerospace Agency reported that combining cold atom accelerometers with force balance accelerometers expanded the measurement range by three orders of magnitude. Around the same time, Tsinghua University reported combining the research approach of classical white-light interferometers with atomic interferometric gyroscopes, significantly enhancing the dynamic range of angular velocity measurement. Most research on entanglement-based quantum measurement focuses on locally measuring the probe and reference signals entangled on a single sensor. However, many future applications may rely on multiple sensors to jointly perform measurement tasks.

Theoretical analysis has shown that interconnecting distributed quantum sensors to form a network of entanglement-based quantum sensors (QSN) can surpass the standard quantum limit (SQL) in measurement precision. The theoretical framework for distributed quantum sensing based on discrete variables (DV) and continuous (CV) entanglement has been proposed. DV-QSN uses entangled discrete photons or atoms as measurement units, with typical applications including entangled quantum clock networks. The atoms within each clock node are first entangled, and then the entangled states are transferred between all clock nodes using QT techniques to achieve global entanglement. Ramsey interferometry can be performed for global frequency synchronization, and various security attacks can be countered using methods such as QKD, random phase modulation, and central-point permutation, resulting in a secure and highly accurate synchronized clock network.

CV-QSN uses entangled squeezed light signals as measurement units and generally applies to amplitude, phase detection, or quantum imaging. In 2020, the University of Arizona in the US reported using CV-QSN for compressed vacuum phase measurements, achieving a measurement variance of 3.2 dB lower than the SQL. It holds promise for exploration in ultra-sensitive positioning, navigation, and timing.

5.5.2 The Gap in Quantum Measurement

However, in many areas of quantum measurement, there is still a significant gap between China's technological research and prototype development and the international advanced level.

Numerous European and US companies have already introduced commercial products based on cold atoms, such as gravity sensors, frequency standards (clocks), accelerometers, and gyroscopes, and actively conducted research and product development in emerging fields, including quantum computing. The industrialization progress has been relatively rapid. Representative quantum sensing and measurement companies include AOSense in the US, an innovative manufacturer of atomic optical sensors specializing in high-precision navigation, time and frequency standards, and gravity measurement research. Their main products include compact commercial quantum gravity sensors and cold atomic frequency standards, and they collaborate with institutions such as NASA in research.

Quspin, also in the US, developed a miniaturized SERF atomic magnetometer in 2013 and released the second-generation product in 2019, with a probe volume of up to 5 cm^3, further advancing toward developing brain magnetometer array systems. Geometrics, another US company, is dedicated to developing seismometers and atomic magnetometers and has launched multiple ground-based and airborne geomagnetic measurement products. Muquans in France has developed an extensive product line in quantum inertial sensing, high-performance timing and frequency applications, and advanced laser solutions. Their main products include absolute quantum gravity sensors and cold atomic frequency standards. In 2020, they began research and development of quantum computing processors. MSquaredLasers in the UK develop inertial sensors for gravity, acceleration, rotation, and quantum timing devices. Their main products include quantum accelerometers, quantum gravity sensors, and optical lattice clocks. They have also ventured into developing neutral atom and ion-based quantum computers.

On the other hand, China's quantum measurement applications and industrialization are still in the early stages and lag behind European and American countries. In the forefront research of optical clocks, China's prototype accuracy is two orders of magnitude lower than the international advanced level. There is still a certain gap in both volume and precision for China's NMR gyro prototypes. There are gaps in the research and systematic integration of quantum target identification. The research on microwave quantum detection technology in China lags significantly behind the leading international level. As for quantum gravity sensors, performance indicators are comparable, but the engineering and development of miniaturized products are still in the early stages.

China's more mature quantum measurement products mainly focus on quantum time-frequency synchronization. Chengdu Tianao is researching and developing time and frequency products and BeiDou satellite application products, with atomic clocks as their main product. In addition, China Electronics Technology Group Corporation, China Aerospace Science and Technology Corporation, China Aerospace Science and Industry Corporation, and some research institutions under China Shipbuilding Heavy Industry Group Corporation are gradually conducting quantum measurement research in their respective advantageous fields.

In recent years, universities and research institutions have gradually increased support for commercializing scientific research results. Originating from the USTC, Guoyao Quantum applies quantum-enhanced technology to laser radar for applications in environmental protection, digital meteorology, aviation safety, smart cities, and more, producing cost-effective quantum detection laser radar. Guoyi Quantum, focusing on quantum precision measurement as its core technology, provides core key devices represented by enhanced quantum sensors and scientific instrument equipment for analysis and testing. Their main products include electron paramagnetic resonance spectrometers, quantum state control and readout systems, quantum diamond atomic force microscopes, quantum diamond single spin spectrometer, etc.

Future Section

TOWARD THE QUANTUM ERA

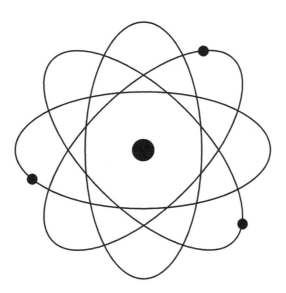

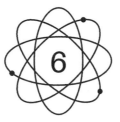

QUANTUM TECHNOLOGY

6.1 Introduction

Today, the second quantum revolution is in full swing.

The first quantum revolution initiated the initial wave of technological advancements based on the principles of quantum mechanics, including lasers, semiconductors, and MRI, among others. Now, a new wave of the quantum revolution focuses on creating a series of disruptive quantum technologies that harness the unique properties of quantum mechanics, such as superposition and entanglement. These technologies provide unprecedented power, precision, security, and sensitivity for quantum applications in communication, computing, radar, timing, sensing, imaging, metrology, and navigation.

6.1.1 The Development of Quantum Science

Currently, quantum science is experiencing rapid global development. On the one hand, the advancement of quantum computing technology is significantly driving the progress of quantum communication. Quantum computing, as a new paradigm that utilizes the principles of quantum mechanics for efficient computation, leverages the superposition properties of quantum states to achieve parallel computations that traditional computers cannot accomplish. Quantum computing holds practical significance for the physical implementation of quantum cryptography, quantum communication, and quantum computers. It has become a research focus in intelligent information processing, particularly in the vast application prospects for information security. The notion that quantum computers are expected to become the next generation is gradually being accepted within the industry.

Quantum technology has made progress in cognitive science, allowing for the emulation of human learning methods within engineering systems and serving the construction of engineering systems that mimic human intelligence. Moreover, optical quantum chips, characterized by high processing speeds and compact sizes, can be applied in the manufacturing of nanoscale robots, various electronic devices, and embedded technologies.

Furthermore, quantum technology applications extend to fields such as satellite spacecraft, nuclear energy control for large-scale equipment, neutrino communication technology, quantum communication technology, and vacuum space communication technology in information dissemination. They also hold immense market potential in advanced military high-tech weaponry and cutting-edge medical research. With advancements in quantum storage capacity, quantum computing technology, and the application of technologies, such as quantum error correction codes and quantum detection, the efficiency of quantum communication systems is expected to greatly improve.

On the other hand, from dedicated networks to public networks, quantum communication is moving toward large-scale applications. Quantum communication technology is a fundamental means of addressing information security and holds significant economic and strategic value. Its long-term goal is to achieve absolute secure long-distance quantum communication, ultimately promoting the industrialization of secure quantum communication. Quantum communication is currently a global focus, progressing from principles to the practical implementation of specialized, small-scale problems.

However, further exploration is required regarding how to integrate quantum communication systems into classical communication networks, how to balance cost and benefits, and how to truly realize a quantum communication network. From the perspective of the quantum communication network system roadmap, the practical application of quantum communication technology will proceed in three steps: first, the realization of regional quantum communication networks through optical fibers; second, the establishment of urban quantum communication networks through quantum relays; and third, the achievement of global wide-area quantum communication networks through satellite relays.

Currently, quantum communication research has entered a critical phase of engineering implementation. With the industrialization of quantum communication technology and the establishment of global wide-area quantum communication networks, quantum communication is expected to move toward large-scale applications in the next ten years. It will become a driving force for various electronic services such as e-government, e-commerce, e-healthcare, biometric transmission, and intelligent transportation systems. It will provide fundamental security services and the most reliable security guarantees for today's information society.

Moreover, quantum communication holds significant application value and prospects in the military, defense, finance, and other information security domains. It can be used for national-level secure communication in military and defense sectors and in government, telecommunications, securities, insurance, banking, industry and commerce, taxation, and finance sectors and departments involving confidential information and documents. Quantum communication is applicable both in civilian and military contexts, and with the integration of satellite devices, its application areas will become broader, more diverse, and deeper. Once successful, quantum communication satellites will open a new chapter in the information technology industry. They will not only bring about a thorough transformation of traditional information industries but also drive emerging information industries, including computer technology, software, satellite communication, databases, consulting services, audio-visual media, and information system construction, with increased efficiency, high speed, large output, and strong security and confidentiality.

In addition, a space race for quantum satellites is also underway. Although the quantum communication industry is still in its early stages of development, satellite communication and space technology, which have already been widely applied, provide a new solution for global quantum communication. This involves combining quantum storage technology with quantum entanglement exchange and purification techniques to create quantum relays. This breakthrough allows for extending quantum communication distance, overcoming the limitations of short-distance communication through fiber optics and terrestrial free-space links, and achieving true global quantum communication.

Countries capable of quantum satellite transmission will have many new advantages, as they can encrypt highly sensitive information. In order to gain an advantage in quantum communication, all countries with vested interests are competing to develop related technologies. Numerous domestic and international research teams are constructing quantum transmission devices suitable for satellite deployment. The space race for quantum satellites will unfold among nations.

It is foreseeable that with the advancement of quantum technology, a series of significant commercial and defense applications will emerge, bringing lucrative market opportunities and disruptive military capabilities.

6.1.2 Quantum Technology as National Strategy

As humanity's ability to observe and control microscopic particle systems based on quantum mechanics continues to break through and improve, the second wave of the quantum technology revolution is approaching. Quantum information science is an emerging interdisciplinary field that combines quantum mechanics with information science and other disciplines. Quantum computing, quantum communication, and quantum measurement are three important areas of development within quantum information science. They will be the focus of technological innovation and industrial upgrading.

Quantum information technology holds scientific and practical value, potentially leading to disruptive technological innovations that challenge and reconstruct traditional information technology systems. Global development and application of quantum information technology have been accelerating in recent years. Major countries have strengthened their layouts and plans in quantum information technology and increased support and investment, launching development strategies and research application project plans. The US, Europe, and Asia all attach great importance to quantum information and consider it a key topic in maintaining national competitiveness. China is also gradually increasing its emphasis on developing quantum information technology and industry.

6.2 The US

The US government has always attached great importance to quantum technology research, considering it a disruptive and strategic technology that will lead the future military revolution. Federal agencies in the US have supported quantum information science significantly over the past 20 years.

6.2.1 The Ten-Year Quantum Program

As early as 2002, the DARPA of the US Department of Defense formulated the "Quantum Information Science and Technology Development Plan" and released version 2.0 in 2004, outlining the main steps and timetable for quantum computing development. This became a crucial factor for the US to establish an early advantage in quantum information in the early 21st century. In 2007, DARPA incorporated quantum technology as a core foundational technology into its strategic planning, with quantum physics becoming one of DARPA's three leading-edge technologies in the strategic investment field set in 2015.

In 2009, the NSTC of the US published "A Federal Vision for Quantum Information Science," recommending that the government strengthen control and utilization of quantum technology. In response, the NSF established an interdisciplinary research program in quantum information science. In July 2016, the NSTC released the report "Advancing Quantum Information Science: National Challenges and Opportunities," analyzing the challenges and measures for US development in the field, as well as the investment focus of major federal agencies in quantum information technology development. As a supplement to the NSTC report, the US Department of Energy (DOE) published the report "Quantum Sensors at the Convergence of Basic Science, Quantum Information Science, and Computing."

Furthermore, in early 2015, the US ARL published the "2015–2019 Technical Implementation Plan," which outlined the research and development goals and infrastructure construction objectives in quantum information science from 2015 to 2030. Since 2016, the Office of the Secretary of Defense has supported the Quantum Science and Engineering Manufacturing Program across all three military branches.

On June 27, 2018, the US House Science Committee officially passed the "NQI Act," initiating the ten-year quantum program in the US. This milestone is considered a significant step in developing quantum research in the country. It signifies the formal involvement of the US federal government in this emerging field, which holds enormous opportunities and the potential to change the landscape of technological and economic competition.

The US government is coordinating its efforts in various aspects, including basic research, talent development, collaboration with industry, infrastructure, national security and economic growth, and international cooperation. It emphasizes basic science and talent while considering future industrialization and supply chains, aiming to create a quantum ecosystem that integrates academia, industry, and research. Corresponding investments and strategic layouts have also been carried out.

Regarding basic research, the "NQI Act" provides a 10-year implementation period for the US National Quantum Program, aiming for substantial breakthroughs in quantum information science after ten years. The act also requires evaluations every five years to adapt the strategic planning according to progress, emphasizing scientific research.

The Quantum Information Science Subcommittee of the NSTC believes that basic science forms the foundation for a nation's prosperity and security. The US post-World War II military and technological dominance can be attributed to its significant scientific investments. There is consensus among academia and the business sector in the US regarding the potential of quantum technology. Therefore, maintaining a leading position in the scientific development of quantum information science is a well-established policy for the country.

To this end, in October 2020, the Quantum Information Science Subcommittee of the NSTC, in collaboration with the White House Office of Science and Technology Policy, released the "Quantum Frontiers Report." Based on the input and expertise of quantum information science experts, this report identified eight key frontiers in quantum information science that the government, private sector, and academia should strive to make breakthroughs in. These frontiers include expanding quantum technology opportunities for societal benefits, establishing the discipline of quantum engineering, materials science for quantum technology, exploring quantum mechanics through quantum simulation, utilizing quantum information technology for precise measurement, generating and distributing quantum entanglement for new applications, characterizing and mitigating quantum biases and errors, and using quantum information science to understand the universe.

In terms of talent development, like other disciplines, the cultivation of talent in quantum information science in the US relies on long-term stable investments in basic research and the creation of job opportunities in universities, laboratories, and related industries. In line with this, the Quantum Information Science Subcommittee of the NSTC has established an interagency workforce working group responsible for engaging with the education sector, industry, and the Quantum Economic Development Consortium (QED-C) and coordinating talent development matters among federal member agencies.

The NSF, NIST, DOE, NASA, and other agencies have established their research centers and programs, each with its talent development plans. In particular, the NSF, a major funder of talent development and recognizing the interdisciplinary nature of quantum information science, has established a working group to facilitate coordination among several of its technology directorates. For example, the Q-12 Education Partnership Program, led by the NSF and the National Quantum Coordination Office, is a public-private collaboration to promote the formation and development of the quantum community. Members of this partnership program are primarily responsible for education and outreach efforts in quantum information science. Teacher training in relevant fields has already begun in the summer of 2021 with support from the NSF and the Q-12 partnership program.

The NIST has also established projects to support graduate students and postdoctoral researchers. For example, it provides support through research institutions established in collaboration with several universities, such as the JILA Institute (jointly established with the University of Colorado), the Joint Quantum Institute (established in partnership with the University of Maryland), and the Joint Center for Quantum Information and Computer Science (established in partnership with the University of Maryland).

The DOE incorporates quantum information science into its Graduate Student Research activities, which are managed by its Office of Science. DOE's national laboratories organize summer schools, internships, and other opportunities to promote and enhance education and training in quantum information science. The DOE actively supports students in quantum information science through programs like the Computational Science Graduate Fellowship.

In collaboration with the industry, the US government has introduced the "NQI Act" and the "NQI Strategic Overview." Both documents recognize the importance of government-industry-academia alliances as crucial mechanisms for promoting the commercialization of emerging technologies, establishing research priorities and directions, and setting standards and regulations. The Quantum Information Science Subcommittee of the NSTC has also established the "End-User Interagency Working Group" to connect developers of quantum information science technologies with potential early adopters. One of the goals of this working group is to help other government departments understand opportunities in quantum information science and develop potential applications. Additionally, the DOE-led Quantum Information Science Centers and the Quantum Leap Challenge Institutes funded by the NSF have industry partnerships facilitating technology commercialization.

Regarding infrastructure development, the Quantum Information Science Center at DOE and the Quantum Leap Challenge Institutes at the NSF represent significant investments in quantum information science infrastructure, as outlined in the "NQI Act."

The Quantum Science Center, led by Oak Ridge National Laboratory, is one such center. It collaborates with 16 institutions, including universities (UC Berkeley, Harvard University, Princeton University, Caltech, University of Washington), national laboratories (Los Alamos National Laboratory, Fermi National Accelerator Laboratory, Pacific Northwest National Laboratory), and companies (Microsoft, IBM), among others. The center focuses on overcoming quantum state restoration, controllability, and scalability obstacles. Oak Ridge National Laboratory has been involved in quantum research for nearly 20 years. It has developed core capabilities in quantum computing, quantum materials, quantum networking, and quantum sensing, achieving significant breakthroughs. These include setting records for quantum information transfer, expanding the range of quantum distribution systems, and collaborating with Google to demonstrate quantum supremacy.

Recognizing the significance of quantum technology for national security and economic growth, the US established the Subcommittee on Economic and

Security Implications of Quantum Sciences (ESIX) under the NSTC. ESIX operates at the same level as the Quantum Information Science Subcommittee and is jointly chaired by the Department of Defense, the National Security Agency, the DOE, and the Office of Science and Technology Policy. It serves as a forum to address economic and national security issues related to quantum information technology.

Several US institutions have embarked on joint projects with international partners regarding international cooperation. For example, the US and Japan jointly signed the "Tokyo Statement on Quantum Cooperation" in December 2019.

The Quantum Information Science Subcommittee of the NSTC, in coordination with the Office of Science and Technology Policy and the US Department of State, promotes international collaboration in quantum information science. Current initiatives include the US-Australia Quantum Industry Dialogue, which brings together representatives from industry, academia, and government to share perspectives on quantum industry competitiveness and foster ways to enhance private-sector collaboration and public-private partnerships between the two sides. The US-UK Quantum Working Group Dialogue brings cross-sector stakeholders from both sides to explore collaboration on everything from basic research to market incubation and talent development. NIST is also involved in developing international quantum information science and technology standards.

6.2.2 Breakthroughs in Quantum Communication

The US started its theoretical and experimental research on quantum communication early on. It was among the first to include it in national strategies, defense, and security research and development programs. For instance, from 1994 to 2014, quantum cryptography research in the US showed a very active trend, progressing from laboratory research to commercial development and product launches, forming an effective industry chain. In order to ensure competitive advantages and maximize the interests of various interest groups in the future communication field, relevant institutions and inventors in the US have been proactively applying for efficient patents, filing patent applications in multiple countries and regions, constructing a patent protection network to cover the widest possible range, and thereby capturing the market for secure communication devices.

The patent applications of quantum communication research institutions in the US have two distinct characteristics. On the one hand, research is primarily conducted in laboratories at universities or research institutes, which have strong theoretical foundations and simultaneously file numerous patent applications. University institutions such as The Johns Hopkins University, the University of Rochester, The Regents of the University of California, and Northwestern University have patents in quantum cryptography.

On the other hand, research-oriented companies play a significant role in developing corresponding methods for quantum cryptographic communication and related communication products to seize market opportunities. For example, MAGIQ, founded in 1999, is a privately held company and the first to focus on commercializing quantum information processing. Through integrating science, business, and engineering technology, MAGIQ seeks to lead the commercialization of quantum information through competitive technological advantages. Its patents in quantum cryptographic communication cover a wide range of technologies, and some patents have been filed in mainland China in recent years.

BBN Technologies Corp is another standout company in terms of patents related to quantum cryptographic communication. The company has significantly contributed to QKD for private communication networks. It has developed highly reliable quantum cryptographic systems for network protection, some of which have been marketed to the military for communication networks.

Other companies such as General Dynamics Advanced Information Systems, Inc., Lucent Technologies Inc., Hewlett-Packard Development Company, L.P., International Business Machines Corporation, and Verizon Corporate Service Group Inc. possess considerable research and development capabilities and have performed well regarding patents. Whether it is basic research on quantum cryptographic communication or the development of related products, the US demonstrates a strong awareness of protecting cutting-edge technologies through patent applications, occupying the field of secure communication with high-end technology. In quantum communication in the US, there is cooperation and competition among patent application institutions or applicants, making the field exceptionally active. There is fierce competition among these institutions or applicants while maintaining close collaboration in the research field.

Patent applications related to quantum cryptographic communication in the US have the characteristics of many patents, frequent citations, a wide distribution of patent holders, and numerous inventors, demonstrating strong capabilities in the quantum cryptographic communication. The development of quantum communication in the US focuses on technological research and application. The quantum cryptographic communication technology level is among the world's best and is used in national-level secure communication for military and defense purposes. It can also be applied in government, telecommunications, securities, insurance, banking, business, local tax, and financial sectors and departments involving confidential data and documents. Today, the quantum communication industry has permeated various aspects of national development in the US, including defense, diplomacy, economy, information, society, and other fields.

At the same time, the US attaches great importance to the expansion of technology in quantum computers. Google, Microsoft, and IBM have been put into research quantum computer technology, quantum computer technology research as a breakthrough point, extended to the material sciences, life sciences, and energy science, to form a scale advantage.

6.3　The EU

Quantum theory originated in Europe, and the EU has always attached great importance to the potential applications of quantum communication technology in national economic security and has invested significant resources in its technological research and development.

Since 1993, research on quantum communication has gradually moved from theory to experimentation and has been advancing toward practical applications. Since 1993, the EU has intensified its efforts in quantum communication and has made breakthroughs in both theoretical and experimental research. The initial focus of the research was on QT, and in 2012, a breakthrough was achieved in the transmission of quantum states, from a 10 km fiber transmission to an invisible transmission over 143 km. From 2007 to 2014, the EU focused on research on quantum cryptographic communication and quantum dense coding, enabling information transfer between Earth and space and making quantum communication between satellites and satellite ground stations possible.

6.3.1 Related Key Policies

The EU's policy planning in quantum technology began in the 1990s, and since then, quantum technology has become a key development direction for the EU.

In March 2016, the European Commission released the "Quantum Manifesto (Draft)" and planned to launch a 1-billion-euro flagship initiative for quantum technology by 2018. The EU strongly supports the development of quantum communication to ensure Europe's technological leadership in this research. The EU has early foundations and ample reserves of basic strength in the research of quantum communication and quantum information technology, which are intertwined with national interests, security, and strategic influences.

In 2017, the EU's flagship initiative for quantum technology announced five main areas, including quantum computing, quantum simulation, quantum sensing and metrology, quantum communication, and fundamental quantum science. Most of the suggestions proposed in the Quantum Manifesto were accepted. Funds for quantum communication were allocated to the Quantum Internet Alliance, which consists of 12 European research institutes and companies dedicated to developing a "QT" network covering the European continent. Funds for quantum computing were allocated to teams researching superconducting circuits and trapped-ion electromagnetic technology. Other approved projects also incorporate the term "Q" (Quantum), such as "PhoQuS" (Photons for Quantum Simulation).

In addition, some of the proposed technologies are closer to market applications, such as ultra-precise and portable atomic clocks, as well as random number generators for secure networks and chip-sized devices.

On April 19, 2018, the European Commission officially announced its support for the Quantum Manifesto initiative and pledged to invest 2 billion euros in cloud computing by 2020. In August 2018, the German federal government also announced a quantum project, planning to invest 650 million euros.

On October 29, 2018, the European Commission announced the first batch of recipients of funds, including 20 international joint research groups consisting of companies and public research institutions. They will receive funding of 132 million euros from the "Horizon 2020" program for a three-year demonstration project.

The period from October 2018 to September 2021 is the initial phase of the Quantum Manifesto initiative (Ramp-up Phase). After 2021, the fund will support an additional 130 projects, covering the entire value chain from basic research to industrialization and bringing together researchers and quantum technology industries.

In May 2020, the flagship program published a strategic research agenda report on its official website, stating its commitment to promoting the construction of a quantum communication network across Europe in the next three years. The report aims to improve and expand existing digital infrastructure to lay the foundation for a future "Quantum Internet."

The short-term goals (3 years) mentioned in the report include considering end-to-end security of the European Quantum Communications Infrastructure (EuroQCI), developing application scenarios and business models, and creating economically efficient and scalable equipment and systems for intercity and intracity usage. The report also emphasizes the development of trusted node networks to enhance interoperability between fiber, free space, and satellite links. It highlights using QKD protocols and satellite-based quantum cryptography for global secure key distribution. Collaboration with European mainstream standardization organizations such as the ETSI is proposed to establish standards for QRNG and QKD authentication methods. Further development of QKD, QRNG, and quantum security certification systems is recommended to prepare for deployment in critical infrastructure, the Internet of Things, and 5G. Achieving end-to-end secure communication on trusted nodes among EU countries is also a priority. The medium to long-term goals (6–10 years) includes demonstrating a series of quantum relays covering significant physical distances (at least 800 km), showcasing quantum network nodes with a minimum of 20 qubits, and demonstrating device-independent QRNG and QKD.

The EU's quantum communication industry is in the mid-stage of technological research and development. It has a considerable grasp of core technologies in the industry. It aims to gain a competitive advantage in technological innovation by focusing on new technology research and marketing new products. EU member states, defense departments, the scientific community, and the information industry have incorporated quantum communication into their defense technology development strategies. They have invested significant human and material resources into quantum communication research, focusing on quantum computing technology, promoting the application of quantum communication in information science, actively constructing and strengthening the industry chain and cluster, and forming an innovation system and scale advantage. Moreover, the scope extends to material, life, and energy science.

6.3.2 Quantum Information Network

Since 1993, the EU has strengthened its research and development efforts in quantum information technology. It has made significant breakthroughs in both theoretical research and experimental technology. The areas covered include quantum cryptographic communication, QT, and quantum dense coding. In the early stages, the focus was mainly on QT, while later stages shifted toward developing vector quantum cryptographic communication and quantum dense coding.

From 1993 to 2012, the EU's quantum remote transmission distance developed from 10 km of fiber optic transmission to 143 km of covert transmission. From 2007 to 2014, the EU began focusing on quantum cryptographic communication and quantum dense coding research, achieving information transmission between quantum walks, space, and Earth, thereby enabling quantum communication between satellites and satellites and ground stations.

Furthermore, since 2000, with the advancement of practical quantum information technology, the EU has further emphasized the technology and its engineering implementation. In October 2008, the EU, along with 41 partner groups from 12 EU countries, invested 14.71 million euros to establish the "SECOQC Project." A secure quantum communication system based on commercial networks was demonstrated in Vienna, Austria.

The system integrated various quantum cryptographic techniques and consisted of six nodes and eight point-to-point QKD connections. The network was structured so that each node utilized multiple QKD send-and-receive systems connected through trusted relays. The network's grid topology did not employ optical routing but relied entirely on trusted intermediate connections. Among the eight connections in the network, seven were optical fiber channels, the longest being 85 km, and one was an 80 m free-space channel.

In 2009, Spanish researchers established a metropolitan quantum communication network testbed, including a backbone network and access networks. The network was integrated into existing optical communication networks, using industrial-grade technologies extensively. The purpose was to investigate the deployment of quantum communication networks within the existing network infrastructure, considering aspects such as traffic flow, limitations, and costs. The backbone network of this quantum network was structured in a ring topology, with quantum channels using a wavelength of 1,550 nm and classical channels using two wavelengths: 1,510 nm and 1,470 nm. The access network utilized the (Gigabit Passive Optical Network) standard. The network employed ID Quantique's QKD system modules 3000 and 3100, with communication using the BB84 with decoy states. The channel tolerated a loss of up to 15 dB, and under this loss, the critical rate was only a few bits per second. In ideal conditions (zero error rate) and considering detector time effects, the maximum rate reached 100 Kb/s.

6.4 The UK

The UK's NQTP is considered the world's first quantum technology program aimed at a broad range of areas, including quantum computing, communication, timing, sensing, and imaging. Today, this program has been imitated by countries worldwide focusing on quantum research.

6.4.1 Four Quantum Technology Hubs

From 2014 to 2024, during NQTP's first and second phases, the UK plans to invest approximately £1 billion in quantum technology research.

Among them, the period from 2014 to 2019 marked the first phase of the NQTP. Initially, the UK established four Quantum Technology Hubs, focusing on quantum computing, quantum communication, quantum-enhanced imaging, and quantum timing and sensing. These hubs were created with a government investment of US$214 million in 2014, with each hub hosted by a university representing a broad range of key areas designated by the national program.

Quantum Computing and Simulation Hub (QCS): The QCS hub is at the University of Oxford. Its mission is to accelerate progress in quantum computing, covering the entire hardware and software stack, from core technologies to potential short- and long-term applications.

Quantum Communications Hub: It is based at the University of York and aims to go beyond the current limitations of prototype quantum security technologies, providing future, practical, and secure communication solutions with commercial potential. The hub focuses on technology applications that rely on QKD.

UK Quantum Technology Sensors and Timing Hub: It is established at the University of Birmingham to develop a range of quantum sensors and measurement techniques.

The UK Quantum Technology Hub in Quantum Enhanced Imaging (QuantIC): QuantIC is located at the University of Glasgow and envisions creating a family of multidimensional cameras spanning wavelengths, time scales, and length scales.

The period from 2019 to 2024 corresponds to the second phase of the NQTP. The NQTP plans to shift its focus and resources toward commercially driven projects during this phase. As products become more market-oriented, the program's partners also seek more control over the emerging plans to ensure they can benefit from the collaborative framework provided by the program.

In return, Innovate UK utilizes the Industrial Strategy Challenge Fund (ISCF) to initiate a series of projects supported by a mix of public and private funding, aiming to support the development of a thriving quantum ecosystem.

The Innovate UK team places great importance on program management and enhancing commercial demonstrations of program initiatives. The focus has shifted to the quantum value chain, and attention to individual qubits and superposition has transitioned to the possibilities of quantum entanglement. Additionally, the UK plans to establish quantum-enhanced imaging as its research pillar. The UK's plan targets opportunities in niche markets, stimulates potential quantum photonics ecosystems, and develops crucial sensing technologies.

The UK National Quantum Computing Center (NQCC) is another major objective of the second phase. The NQCC does not envision becoming a direct competitor in the quantum computing race but rather as a tool to accelerate societal efficiency. The design of the physical center has been completed, and construction work will continue until 2021–2022, with plans for delivery and utilization in the first quarter of 2023. Initially, the center prioritizes superconducting qubits, ion traps, and software research. Still, the funds allocated to the center are for investments in the quantum field rather than specific quantum technologies.

Furthermore, the ISCF funds over 40 quantum projects initiated in three important quantum research areas. Typically, each consortium consists of 3–10 partners from across the supply chain and offers strong academic support. Projects are usually set to run for 18–36 months with budgets ranging from £5–10 million. This approach provides flexibility for supplementary projects in subsequent developments while supporting various project types.

6.4.2 Talent Development in the Quantum Program

Talent development is another key focus of the UK Quantum Program.

QTEC, a program from the first phase of the UK NQTP, aids scientists in their transition to becoming entrepreneurs. The "Fellowship" provides early-stage researchers with salary, expenses, business training, and guidance, offering them a one-year entrepreneurial journey.

Early-stage researchers from QTEC are involved in training initiatives from emerging players in the quantum field, such as KETS and Seeqc, or they have made notable progress in commercial applications within specific areas, such as QLM or FluoretiQ. Two recent notable startups are Nu Quantum and Quantum Dice. Fact Based Insight suggests that QTEC has achieved significant success.

However, the second phase of the NQTP currently lacks funding for its continuation. The initial funding came from the Engineering and Physical Sciences Research Council (EPSRC), but the EPSRC's core objectives are focused on scientific research and training. Meanwhile, Innovate UK has been actively initiating ISCF projects. Fact Based Insight hopes that the NQTP can proceed with its second phase. The NQTP aims to make the UK an ideal place for quantum businesses and talent. Previously, PsiQ relocated to Silicon Valley due to difficulties obtaining research funding in Europe.

During the second phase of the NQTP, the UK Quantum Program has achieved significant accomplishments. US companies such as Rigetti and Cold Quanta have also been attracted to the UK's quantum research environment. Teledyne e2v and Hitachi have expanded their research and development bases in the field through their subsidiaries in the UK. Toshiba manufactures QKD devices in the UK. It can be said that a vibrant quantum research environment has begun to take shape in the UK.

6.5 Japan

The Japanese government considers quantum technology a priority high-tech field in which the country has a certain advantage. They focus on guiding the development of related cutting-edge technologies in Japan.

6.5.1 The Research of Related Cutting-Edge Technologies

Since 2001, Japan has formulated long-term research strategies and development roadmaps for next-generation quantum information communication technology. Through intensive research and development investments, they have adopted a collaborative approach involving industry, government, and academia to advance key technologies in quantum communication. This includes pursuing ultra-high-speed computers, quantum optical transmission, and unbreakable optical quantum cryptography, aiming for practical applications and engineering exploration.

The Ministry of Posts and Telecommunications in Japan has identified quantum information as a national strategic project for the 21st century. They have specifically formulated a ten-year medium- to long-term research objective, aiming to achieve practical levels of secure communication network and quantum communication network technologies by 2020. Ultimately, they aim to establish a nationwide high-speed quantum communication network, enabling a leap forward in communication technology and gaining a competitive advantage.

In December 2011, Japan established the "Optical and Quantum Beam Research and Development Task Committee" under the Council for Science and Technology Policy. This committee discusses the current research status and domestic and international situations regarding quantum optical technology and deliberates on strategic policy directions for ongoing and future projects. In 2016, the Japanese Cabinet positioned "Light/Quantum Technology" as one of the foundational technologies for creating core value in the "Fifth Science and Technology Basic Plan (2016–2020)." In February 2017, the Quantum Technology Committee, a subsidiary of the Council for Science and Technology Policy, published a midterm report titled "Latest Promotion Directions for Quantum Science and Technology," highlighting the key development directions Japan should focus on in this field.

Japan plans to establish a secure and confidential high-speed quantum communication network by 2020–2030, achieving a qualitative leap in communication technology applications. The National Institute of Information and Communications Technology (NICT) in Japan plans to achieve quantum relay in 2020 and establish a wide-area optical fiber and free-space quantum communication network with ultimate capacity and unconditionally secure communications by 2040.

6.5.2 The Development of Related Research

Although Japan started its research on quantum communication technology later than the US and the EU, it has experienced rapid development. With the support and guidance of national science and technology policies and strategic plans, Japanese research institutions have shown high enthusiasm for research and development. They have invested significant research capital and actively participated in and undertaken research on quantum communication technology. Moreover, they have made substantial progress in quantum communication technology research and industrial development. Major companies and research institutions in Japan, such as NEC, Toshiba, the NICT, the University of Tokyo, Tamagawa University, Hitachi, Panasonic, NTT, Mitsubishi, Fujitsu, Canon, JST, and others, lead the world in terms of patent applications in quantum communication. They have high-quality patents and outstanding technological capabilities.

Japan's research advantage in quantum communication focuses on extending the distance of quantum communication transmission, improving information transmission speed, and enhancing quantum communication encryption protocols. The main characteristics of quantum communication patents filed by Japanese companies include a wide range of application technologies, high patent ownership rates in specific technical fields, strong awareness of filing international patents, and the direct applicability of related technologies to communication products, demonstrating the practicality and market potential.

Moreover, Japan emphasizes adopting an active patent protection strategy to safeguard its core quantum communication technologies through the comprehensive filing of Patent Cooperation Treaty patents. Japanese companies are officially launching the development of "quantum computers," which will have computing speeds far surpassing existing computers. NEC is researching and developing the fundamental circuitry equivalent to the brain of a quantum computer and aims to achieve practicality as early as 2023. Fujitsu plans to invest 50 billion yen in developing related technologies over the next three years.

While Japanese companies are ahead in basic research, they are relatively lagging in commercialization. Starting in the 2018 fiscal year, the Japanese government has strengthened its support for universities and other institutions in research and development, aiming to achieve collaboration between industry, government, and academia. Quantum computers utilize physical phenomena such as electrons and can instantly solve problems that would take thousands of years for supercomputers to unravel. They have the potential to significantly enhance AI, analyze DNA, and optimize efficient routes for autonomous driving vehicles, among other new value-creation possibilities.

NEC's "quantum annealing" approach derives the most suitable answer from many options. The company is currently working on producing the fundamental circuitry and plans to invest billions of yen in developing physical machines before 2023. NEC's technology achieves a computational capacity of 2,000–3,000 qubits, rapidly selecting the most suitable traffic routes for hundreds of cities at various times. Regarding quantum annealing, NEC's technology surpasses that of the leading Canadian company, D-Wave Systems, which has a capacity of around 2,000 qubits.

NEC states that their performance will be even higher, even with the same number of qubits. They aim to advance collaboration between industry, government, and academia to increase the computational capacity to 10,000 qubits within ten years. Fujitsu plans to invest 50 billion yen in developing quantum computer-related technologies before the end of the 2020 fiscal year. They will promote basic research by dispatching personnel to active quantum computer research centers like the University of Toronto in Canada. Fujitsu also plans to engage in capital cooperation with 1QBit, a Canadian company developing quantum computer software, and expand businesses' adoption of related technologies.

In quantum computers, companies like D-Wave and IBM in the US have already entered the commercialization phase, and Japanese companies are also beginning to explore implementation. Companies like NEC started developing quantum computers over 20 years ago but were surpassed by overseas companies in practical applications. Well-funded American companies like Google are advancing the development of more versatile "quantum gate" approaches. IBM has been providing related services through the cloud since 2017 and is also working on prototype development. To counteract this, NTT began offering free public access to prototype machines utilizing the quantum properties of light in November 2017. They aim to increase the computational capacity of quantum computers from the current 4,000 qubits to 100,000 qubits in the future.

6.6 China

China has gradually increased its attention and support to quantum information technology to take advantage of the second quantum technology revolution. With many investments, China has gained an explosive development of quantum technology.

6.6.1 Policies, Funding, and Talent

Based on China's high regard for basic research, scientific experiments, demonstration applications, network infrastructure, and industrial cultivation of quantum information technology, the Ministry of Science and Technology and the Chinese Academy of Sciences provide support for explorations in fundamental research and applications of quantum information through various scientific projects such as the National Natural Science Foundation, the "863" Program, the "973" Program, the National Key R&D Program, and the Strategic Priority Research Program. The NDRC leads the implementation of pilot projects and network construction, including the quantum secure communication "Beijing–Shanghai Trunk Line" and the National Backbone Quantum Secure Communication Network. The Ministry of Industry and Information Technology organizes research on the application and industrial development of quantum secure communication and support. It guides the standardization of research and collaborative innovation among academia, industry, and research institutions in quantum information technology.

During the Academicians Conference of the Chinese Academy of Sciences and the Academicians Conference of the Chinese Academy of Engineering in May 2018, President Xi Jinping emphasized the acceleration of breakthrough applications in new-generation information technologies represented by AI, quantum information, mobile communications, the Internet of Things, and blockchain. The strategic position of quantum information was further affirmed.

On October 16, 2020, the 24th collective study session of the Political Bureau of the CPC Central Committee focused on quantum technology's research and application prospects. General Secretary Xi Jinping delivered an important speech, providing strategic planning and systematic arrangements for developing quantum technology in China in the current and future. The speech fully recognized the significant innovative achievements of Chinese scientists in quantum technology and pointed out the shortcomings, risks, and challenges for future development. The speech outlined a comprehensive and systematic layout for developing quantum technology in China from five aspects: trend analysis, top-level design planning, policy guidance and support, talent cultivation and incentives, and collaborative innovation among academia, industry, and research institutions. It further provided direction for grasping the overall trend and making proactive moves.

In the "14th Five-Year Plan" proposal released during the Fifth Plenary Session of the 19th CPC Central Committee on November 3 of the same year, it was further suggested to focus on frontier areas such as AI, quantum information, integrated circuits, life and health, brain science, biological breeding, aerospace technology, deep underground, and deep sea. Several forward-looking and strategic national major scientific and technological projects will be implemented. Compared to other countries, mainland China has made significant investments in quantum science and technology research. According to statistics, China's investment in this field is second only to the US.

In addition to government efforts, private enterprises also attach great importance to developing quantum science and technology. In today's knowledge-based economy, being at the forefront of technology and innovation means enormous economic benefits and even the ability to capture market share. Examples abound, such as the highly sought-after iPhones. Furthermore, the rapid development and constant upgrading of information transmission and electronic science and technology pose significant business challenges. Intense market competition has prompted companies to focus more on technological breakthroughs and innovations to avoid being phased out by society. In China, many technology giants have shown interest in quantum science and technology, such as Alibaba, which committed to quantum computing research, and Huawei, which has achieved breakthrough innovations in 5G technology through quantum communication.

In addition to sufficient funding support, China also places great emphasis on talent cultivation. In quantum science research, many universities have established mature teams with prestigious researchers, such as the team led by Pan Jianwei. The Science Development Report also highlights the importance of the development of quantum communication science, and there are numerous related laboratories to facilitate research by scientists.

6.6.2 The Leapfrog Development of Quantum Technology

With significant investments, China's quantum technology has experienced explosive development, which is even regarded as a leapfrog development by the world.

As early as 2003, the team led by Pan Jianwei at the USTC proposed a scheme to realize inter-satellite quantum communication and construct a global quantum secure communication network. This scheme was officially approved at the end of 2011 and took a milestone step on August 16, 2016: China successfully launched the world's first quantum science experimental satellite, "Micius."

It is worth mentioning that prior to 2016, China seemed to have limited achievements and breakthroughs in quantum science theory. However, since the launch of "Micius," the first quantum satellite in the world, in 2016, China's development in quantum science has been increasingly remarkable, with more and more groundbreaking inventions. Based on the "Micius" satellite, the team led by Pan Jianwei completed three major scientific experiments in August 2017, more than a year ahead of schedule. This marked China's pioneering mastery of the technology for satellite-to-ground wide-area quantum communication networks.

On September 29, 2017, China opened the world's first quantum secure communication trunk line, the "Beijing–Shanghai Trunk Line." This quantum communication secure trunk line spans over 2,000 km, connecting Beijing and Shanghai via Jinan and Hefei, with 32 quantum communication nodes.

However, although the encryption in quantum communication is unbreakable, the communication nodes can be compromised. Attacking the source end of the nodes makes it possible to steal the quantum encryption. In simple terms, physical means attack the devices required for quantum communication rather than mathematically decrypting the codes. In other words, the "Beijing–Shanghai Trunk Line" has theoretical vulnerabilities at the engineering level. Of course, such vulnerabilities can be addressed through engineering means, such as enhancing device security.

There are security risks in using "Micius" for quantum communication. When using conventional transmission methods for information transfer, the "Micius" satellite holds all the keys distributed by users. If other parties control the satellite, there is a risk of information leakage. However, Pan Jianwei and his team addressed this issue with an achievement published in *Nature* in June 2020.

By utilizing the characteristic of quantum entanglement, Pan Jianwei's team only performs measurements on the quantum at the user end of the ground station, ensuring that the entanglement source (the satellite) does not possess any key information. The keys will not be leaked even if other parties hijack the satellite. Before this research paper, the efficiency and error rate of QKD based on satellite entanglement were insufficient to support secure QKD. However, Pan Jianwei's team solved the problem of low efficiency in satellite entanglement distribution by employing special designs and upgrading the main optical and back optical paths of ground station telescopes.

In the end, with the help of "Micius," they successfully achieved entanglement-based QKD between two ground stations separated by 1,120 km. Even under extreme circumstances where the satellite is controlled by other parties, secure quantum communication can still be realized based on physical principles. The evaluation of this achievement by reviewers of *Nature* was: "This is an important step toward building a global QKD network, or even a quantum Internet."

"The Beijing–Shanghai Trunk Line" and "Micius" signify that China has initially constructed the infrastructure for a nationwide integrated quantum communication network. Building upon this foundation, China has been able to drive the industrial application of quantum communication technology.

The "Beijing–Shanghai Trunk Line" has already been used for encrypted data transmission in fields such as finance, government, and national defense. Some Internet companies can also utilize Alibaba Cloud to access cloud-based quantum communication encryption services.

The industrialization of "Micius" presents relatively higher challenges. In the past, the ground stations used in conjunction with "Micius" were bulky and weighed over ten tons, making it difficult for industrial applications. However, on December 30, 2019, China achieved a breakthrough in the commercialization of quantum technology by successfully docking the first miniaturized and mobile quantum satellite ground station (weighing only over 80 kg) with "Micius." This development paves the way for the industrialization of Chinese quantum communication.

During constructing the "Micius" and "Beijing–Shanghai Trunk Line" projects, Pan Jianwei's team also established a commercial company called Guodun Quantum through technology transfer. Since 2017, the US has included key technologies, products, and devices related to quantum communication on its export control list. Guodun Quantum aims to ensure the supply of critical components for the projects through independent research and development. In July 2020, Guodun Quantum became the first publicly listed "quantum communication" company in the A-share market, and its closing price on the first day of trading increased tenfold compared to the issue price, demonstrating the Chinese capital market's enthusiasm for quantum communication technology. However, overall, quantum communication is still a new technology and is currently in the stage of product promotion.

The research achievements in Chinese quantum science and technology have caused significant shock in society and internationally. People have become interested in this once highly mysterious discipline. Private entrepreneurs have spontaneously provided funding to support the development of quantum science and technology. Even local governments have integrated quantum science and technology with regional economic development. Among them, entrepreneurs have donated a billion yuan to establish the Micius Quantum Science and Technology Foundation, which aims to recognize scientists who have made outstanding contributions to quantum science and technology and contribute to its development. The vibrant development of quantum science and technology and its role in economic development has led local governments to increasingly value the application of this scientific technology. They have plans to leverage quantum technology's fast-paced progress for better innovation and regional economic growth. For example, in Hefei, Anhui Province, numerous quantum science and technology companies exist in the High-Tech Zone. Apart from Guodun Quantum, over 20 quantum-related enterprises have emerged.

6.7 Global Companies and Quantum Technology

6.7.1 Google

Google has been focused on the development of practical applications for quantum technology. In 2009, Google began exploring quantum computing, and in 2013, it purchased the world's first commercially available quantum computer from the Canadian startup D-Wave Systems. It then collaborated with NASA's Ames Research Center to establish the Quantum AI Laboratory (QuAIL) using the D-Wave machine to explore the applications of quantum computing in various fields, including network search, speech/image pattern recognition, planning and scheduling, and air traffic management.

In 2013, Google spent approximately US$8 billion on quantum computing research, but there were no significant breakthroughs. In 2014, Google continued its research in quantum computing and announced a collaboration with experts from the University of California, Santa Barbara, to develop quantum computing. They equipped themselves with the latest generation quantum computer, the D-Wave 2X, and built a 9-qubit computer. Google aimed to bridge the gap between machine learning and human intelligence and maintain its leading position in the emerging field of AI. In 2015, Hartmut Neven, the head of QuAIL, and his team published a paper stating that preliminary test results showed that the D-Wave quantum computer could perform certain calculations 100 times faster than traditional computer chips.

In March 2018, Google's QuAIL announced the development of a new 72-qubit quantum processor called Bristlecone, which provided a compelling proof-of-principle for building large-scale quantum computers. This processor was a significant improvement compared to Google's previous 9-qubit processor. Later in 2018, Google announced a partnership with NASA to explore the application scenarios of the new quantum processor.

In 2019, at the IEEE International Solid-State Circuits Conference held in San Francisco, Google showcased a custom-designed circuit for quantum computing. This circuit could operate within a low-temperature enclosure cooled to below 1 kelvin, providing crucial infrastructure for scaling up quantum computer systems in the future.

In the same year, Google computer scientists published a paper on the NASA website, stating that they had achieved a task using a 53-qubit quantum computer that would take the world's most powerful supercomputer, Summit, 10,000 years to complete. Google's quantum computer accomplished the task in just 3 minutes and 20 seconds. This demonstrated that quantum computers outperformed classical computers, and Google researchers declared the achievement of "quantum supremacy."

In March 2020, Google released an open-source library for quantum machine learning called Tensor Flow Quantum. It provides researchers and developers a pathway to use open-source frameworks and computing capabilities. Google is committed to building dedicated quantum hardware and software to help researchers and developers address current theoretical and practical problems and advance the development of quantum computing.

On January 14, 2022, according to Business Insider, Google's parent company, Alphabet, announced the spin-off of its quantum technology team called Sandbox into an independent quantum technology company. Google co-founder Sergey Brin founded Sandbox and is currently led by Jack Hidary. With the spin-off, the organizational structure of the new company is expected to change. Sandbox was regarded as a mysterious quantum computing team within Google because it was not publicly known until 2020. The Sandbox team worked in the X Building and consisted of former employees of Google X, the company's innovation laboratory. The team focuses on developing quantum computing software and experimental quantum projects. As Hidary stated, Sandbox is an "enterprise solution at the intersection of quantum physics and AI."

In addition, this year, Google's Quantum AI team has completed a 16-qubit chemical simulation on the "Sycamore" quantum computer. This is the largest-scale chemical simulation conducted on a quantum computer. The team has proposed a scalable and noise-resistant quantum-classical hybrid algorithm that embeds specialized quantum primitives into precise quantum computing many-body methods, namely the Fermionic Monte Carlo (QMC). They performed unbiased, constrained QMC calculations on a chemical system with up to 16 qubits and 120 orbitals. Their work provides a computational strategy that effectively eliminates biases in Fermionic QMC methods by leveraging state-of-the-art quantum information tools. Finally, they demonstrated its performance in a 16-qubit experiment on a NISQ processor, achieving electron energies comparable to state-of-the-art classical quantum chemistry methods.

6.7.2 Amazon

Amazon provides comprehensive management services that allow users to explore and design quantum algorithms. Users can test their algorithms on Amazon's simulator and run them on different quantum hardware technologies of their choice, thereby aiding in the development of quantum computing.

As the world's largest cloud computing provider, in December 2019, Amazon officially entered the field of quantum cloud computing by launching a new fully managed Amazon Web Services (AWS) solution called Amazon Braket. Braket allows developers, researchers, and scientists to explore, evaluate, and experiment with quantum computing. It enables users to design their quantum algorithms from scratch or choose from pre-built algorithm libraries. Once the algorithms are defined, Amazon Braket provides a fully managed simulation service for debugging and verification.

The Amazon quantum computing cloud platform can connect to various third-party quantum hardware devices such as IonQ's trapped-ion quantum devices, Rigetti's superconducting quantum devices, and D-Wave's quantum annealing devices. It provides researchers and developers with a development environment for designing quantum algorithms, a simulation environment for testing algorithms, and a platform for comparing the performance of quantum algorithms on the three types of quantum computing devices.

As of now, the Braket platform has integrated quantum computing hardware, including D-Wave Quantum Annealing Systems, IonQ ion trap quantum computers, Rigetti quantum processors, OQC superconducting quantum computers, Xanadu photonic quantum computers, QuEra quantum computers, and more. The quantum ecosystem has taken shape.

AWS continues to expand the impact of its quantum program.

In June 2022, Amazon announced the establishment of the Center for Quantum Networking (CQN) in Boston, an important component of Amazon's quantum computing puzzle. The center is dedicated to addressing fundamental scientific and engineering challenges in quantum networking and developing new hardware, software, and applications for quantum networks. Many of the new team members will be based in the Boston area of the US.

Although specific product information has yet to be announced, the CQN center stated they would consider a range of quantum networking and quantum security products, including hardware, software, applications, and various quantum-resistant encryption products. Researchers at the AWS CQN will delve into new technologies, such as quantum relays and sensors, to create a global quantum network that achieves further advancements in privacy, security, and computational capabilities.

6.7.3 IBM

IBM, as one of the leaders in quantum computing, has been involved in quantum computing research for over 30 years and continues to explore new quantum algorithms through fundamental quantum information science research.

In 2016, IBM introduced the IBM 6-qubit prototype and developed a 5-qubit quantum computer for researchers. They launched the world's first quantum computing cloud platform. In 2017, IBM announced the implementation of a 20-qubit quantum computer based on superconducting technology and built a 50-qubit quantum computer as a prototype. In September 2019, they announced the development of a 53-qubit quantum computer. In August 2020, using their latest 27-qubit processor, they achieved a QV of 64.

IBM introduced "QV" as a dedicated metric to measure the performance of quantum computers. Factors affecting QV include the number of qubits, measurement errors, device cross-communication and connectivity, circuit software compilation efficiency, and more. The larger the QV, the more powerful the quantum computer's performance and the more practical problems it can solve.

In 2017, IBM's Tenerife device (5-qubit) achieved a QV of 4. In 2018, the IBM Q device (20-qubit) had a QV of 8. In 2019, the latest IBM Q System One (20-qubit) reached a QV of 16. In 2020, using their latest 27-qubit "Falcon" processor, the QV of their quantum computer increased from 32 to 64 compared to the previous year. Since 2017, IBM has doubled the QV every year.

In 2021, IBM introduced a 127-qubit processor, surpassing Google and USTC. IBM named the 127-qubit superconducting quantum processor "Eagle." The "Eagle" processor is an architectural improvement based on previous advancements and adopts more advanced 3D packaging technology to double the number of qubits. The improvements in "Eagle" include reducing the design of error-prone qubit arrangements and minimizing the required components.

Furthermore, IBM utilizes new technology to place control wiring on multiple physical layers within the processor while keeping the qubits on a single layer, significantly increasing the number of qubits. The more qubits there are, the more complex and valuable quantum circuits it can run. IBM states that "Eagle" can take the complexity of human exploratory problems to the next level, such as optimizing machine learning and providing new molecular and material modeling for various fields from the energy industry to the drug discovery process. Currently, the 127-qubit "Eagle" is the first quantum processor of such scale that classical computers cannot reliably simulate.

Alongside announcing the 127-qubit "Eagle" processor, IBM also introduced their upcoming quantum system, Quantum System 2. Compared to the first generation, launched in 2019 as the world's first integrated quantum computing system, Quantum System 2 adopts a more modular design. It introduces new scalable quantum bit control electronics and higher-density cryogenic components and cables, enabling the accommodation and cooling of more quantum processors in a single system. It will be launched in 2023 and can accommodate new processors with a higher number of qubits in the future.

While making breakthroughs in quantum technology, IBM is also dedicated to building quantum hardware and platform systems for research and commercial purposes. Their research in quantum cloud computing has a systematic and mature research and development model. They have formed a relatively complete research and development chain in both hardware and software, gradually establishing a mature quantum cloud computing ecosystem.

In January 2019, IBM unveiled the world's first commercially available quantum computing system at CES, IBM Q System One. It provided the "highest QV to date," marking the first time a universal approximate superconducting quantum computer was made available outside the laboratory. Users could access the system through the cloud. IBM stated that it would focus on utilizing this system for researching financial data, logistics, and risk.

In June 2019, IBM announced collaborations with several universities in Africa. As part of the partnership, IBM aimed to apply the Q System One to research in various fields, including drug development, mining, and natural resource management. They emphasized that IBM Q could assist users in discovering early use cases, equipping organizations with practical quantum skills, and accessing world-class expertise and technical services to promote the practical use of quantum computing. Recently, Norishige Morimoto, IBM's Global Vice President, stated that IBM plans to commercialize quantum computers within five years.

IBM's Q Network has attracted numerous enthusiastic partners, including top universities and globally renowned technology companies. They collaborate to advance fundamental quantum computing research and make an impact on the real world. Working alongside experimental, theoretical, and computer science experts, they explore new possibilities in quantum computing.

6.7.4 Microsoft

Microsoft began its foray into quantum computing technology in 2005, proposing a method for building topologically protected quantum bits in a hybrid semiconductor-superconductor structure. In December 2011, the QuArC group was formed, which worked on designing software architectures and algorithms for a scalable, fault-tolerant quantum computer. In 2014, Microsoft revealed that its Station Q group is working on topological quantum computing. In 2016, it announced plans to spend significant resources on developing a prototype quantum computer.

Microsoft has also made a strong push in quantum software development and software community operation. Microsoft debuted a new quantum programming language Q#, building a set of independent and better adapted quantum computing programming models, hoping to provide developers with better quantum computing development tools.

Initially, the quantum ecosystem was built around QDK to guide users to use Q#. In late 2017, Microsoft announced the quantum development kit, which allows developers to write applications for quantum computers. In February 2019, Microsoft launched the "Microsoft Quantum Network," a network of organizations and individuals working on quantum applications and hardware. In May 2019, Microsoft said its quantum development kit had reached 100,000 downloads. In July 2019, Microsoft officially open-sourced the QDK, which has all the tools and resources users need to start learning and building quantum solutions, providing a more comprehensive development environment.

Microsoft is one of the few quantum systems companies building on the revolutionary topological quantum bits of the future, and the launch of the AzureQuantum cloud platform unites other quantum companies further to provide quantum hardware services to users across the industry. In November 2019, Microsoft launched Quantum Cloud Ecosystem Services—Azure Quantum, which provides developers and customers with pre-built solutions, software, and quantum hardware. Azure Quantum is the world's first complete, open cloud ecosystem.

6.7.5 Tencent

Although Chinese technology companies entered the field of quantum computing relatively late compared to the US, industry-leading companies and research institutions in China have also started to make layouts in quantum computing in recent years.

Tencent entered the quantum computing field in 2017 and proposed the "ABC2.0" technological layout, which stands for AI, Robotics, and Quantum Computing. Tencent aimed to use AI, robotics, and quantum computing to build future-oriented infrastructure and explore and promote technological services for B-end industries. In 2018, Tencent established Tencent Quantum Laboratory and invited Zhang Shengyu, a quantum computing scientist from the Chinese University of Hong Kong, as the laboratory director.

Tencent is conducting fundamental research in quantum computing, establishing platforms for quantum system development, and exploring the practical implementation of related industries. The fundamental quantum computing theory research directions include quantum combinatorial algorithms, quantum AI, quantum system simulation, and applications in fields such as drug discovery and materials. Results in the direction of quantum combinatorial algorithms include exponential acceleration algorithms for fundamental core problems such as graph connectivity and finding connected subgraphs. Results in quantum AI theory include the development of the first provable quantum square speedup algorithm for general neural networks. In terms of chemical applications, they have achieved effective predictions of the optical absorption properties of organic luminescent materials.

On the one hand, Tencent is also exploring the application of quantum computing technology in enterprise development and finding suitable scenarios for commercial applications, aiming to tangibly promote industrial development through quantum computing. Tencent Quantum Laboratory's technological research and practical explorations have achieved milestone results in chemistry and drug discovery. For example, they have introduced a quantum + AI model into the small molecule drug discovery process, combining quantum computation and discriminative, generative, and reinforcement learning models of machine learning to effectively bridge the gap between the academic community and traditional pharmaceutical companies, helping upgrade traditional drug discovery processes and improve efficiency.

On the other hand, Tencent has adopted a more open approach toward ecological partners. Tencent Quantum Laboratory planned to release an elastic first-principles cloud computing platform in 2021. On the one hand, they will consolidate various software tools in the cloud and provide efficient one-stop services by integrating their self-developed visualization output capabilities. On the other hand, they will adjust the cloud-based system to align cloud services with the habits and scenarios of scientific computing. In the future, the cloud platform will deploy more modules, such as molecular drug properties, activity, quantum system simulation, and developing related AI models. They aim to promote algorithm dissemination, facilitate scientific research collaboration, and establish a cloud-based quantum technology ecosystem.

In January 2022, Tencent announced its latest research in quantum computing, achieving the shortcut for the first time for the adiabatic evolution of open quantum systems. Unlike Alibaba, Tencent Laboratory is developing computational chemistry software and platforms on Tencent Cloud, establishing an ecosystem in quantum chemistry, pharmaceuticals, materials, energy, and other fields.

6.7.6 Huawei

Huawei has been involved in quantum computing research since 2012. Quantum computing is an important research area within Huawei Central Research Institute Data Center Laboratory, focusing on quantum computing software, quantum algorithms, and applications.

At the Huawei Connect 2018 conference, Huawei unveiled its quantum computing simulator, the HiQ Cloud Service Platform. It features a quantum circuit simulator and a quantum programming framework based on the simulator. The HiQ quantum computing simulator includes a full-amplitude simulator providing 42-qubit simulation services and a single-amplitude simulator providing 169-qubit simulation services. Additionally, a quantum error correction simulator capable of simulating hundreds of thousands of qubits was added, marking the industry's first inclusion of this functionality in a cloud service. The HiQ quantum programming framework supports more than ten algorithms and is compatible with the open-source framework ProjectQ. It also introduces two graphical user interfaces, the Quantum Circuit Composition GUI and the Hybrid Composition BlockUI, making classical quantum hybrid programming more straightforward and intuitive.

At Huawei Connect 2019, Huawei introduced the HiQ 2.0 quantum computing software solution. It launched the industry's first all-in-one quantum chemistry application cloud service and HiQ Fermion software package. The update also included cloud-based pulse optimization design services, the HiQ Pulse software package, and the quantum chip control module, HiQ Pulse. These enhancements significantly improved the performance of the quantum computing simulator, optimized quantum algorithms and pulse libraries, expanded the functionality of the quantum computing programming framework, and established an industry-leading framework and simulator cloud service. HiQ 2.0 had a more specialized focus than version 1.0, mainly emphasizing quantum chemistry and quantum control to assist quantum developers in making breakthroughs in pharmaceuticals and materials.

At Huawei Connect 2020, Huawei unveiled the HiQ 3.0 quantum computing simulator and developer tools. It introduced two core modules: the quantum CO solver, HiQ Optimizer, and the tensor network computing accelerator, HiQ Tensor. These additions further enhanced the functionality of the HiQ system and made it adaptable to multiple application scenarios.

As a solid step in Huawei's fundamental research in quantum computing, the cloud service platform utilizes computing, networking, storage, security, and other resources provided by Huawei Cloud. It empowers scientific research and education, enabling quantum computing on regular computers and providing developers with a favorable programming experience. This initiative advances collaboration with partners in exploring and applying quantum computing in various industries.

6.7.7 Alibaba

Alibaba's quantum computing strategy involves two main aspects: establishing laboratories for full-stack hardware-centric research and building an ecosystem through collaboration with partners across the entire industry chain to explore practical applications.

As early as July 2015, Alibaba Cloud partnered with the Chinese Academy of Sciences to establish the "Chinese Academy of Sciences-Alibaba Quantum Computing Laboratory" in Shanghai. This laboratory combines Alibaba Cloud's technical expertise in classical algorithms, architecture, and cloud computing with the Chinese Academy of Sciences strengths in quantum computing, simulation, quantum AI, and other areas. The laboratory focuses on researching the application of quantum computing in various fields, such as AI, e-commerce, and data center security.

In March 2017, Alibaba Cloud announced the world's first case of quantum encryption communication in the cloud. In May of the same year, Alibaba announced the development of its first optical quantum computer, achieving ten qubits. Also in 2017, Alibaba's research institute, DAMO Academy, established a quantum laboratory and invited Shi Yaoyun, a computer science graduate from Peking University and a computer science PhD from Princeton University, as well as a professor at the University of Michigan Ann Arbor, to join as the Chief Scientist of Alibaba Cloud Quantum Technology. Dr. Shi is responsible for establishing and leading the Alibaba Cloud Quantum Computing Laboratory.

In February 2018, the Chinese Academy of Sciences announced a collaboration with Alibaba Cloud to build a cloud platform for 11-qubit superconducting quantum computing, serving as a powerful tool for auxiliary algorithms and hardware design. In May, the laboratory developed a quantum circuit simulator called "Taizhang," which became the world's first simulator to successfully simulate an 81-qubit, 40-layer benchmark random quantum circuit. Previously, simulators with the same number of layers could only handle 49 qubits. In September 2019, the quantum laboratory achieved the development of the first controllable qubit, independently completing its design, fabrication, and measurement. This milestone demonstrated that DAMO Academy has the full capability for the entire chain of research and development in superconducting quantum chips.

Alibaba was the first Chinese technology company to participate in quantum computing and has increasingly emphasized its importance. DAMO Academy named quantum computing one of the top ten technology trends for 2020. In March 2020, Alibaba DAMO Academy launched the Nanhui Project with a total investment of approximately 20 billion RMB, with a primary research focus on quantum computing. In June, Alibaba Innovation Research Program included quantum computing for the first time.

In March 2022, Alibaba participated in the Global Physical Year Meeting and shared its latest quantum achievements. They successfully designed and manufactured a two-qubit quantum chip with a manipulation accuracy surpassing 99.72%, achieving the world's best performance for this type of qubit.

6.7.8 Baidu

In March 2018, Baidu announced the establishment of the Baidu Quantum Computing Institute. Leveraging its strong technological capabilities, including core businesses like cloud computing, Baidu invited Duan Runyao, the founding director of the Center for Quantum Software and Information at the University of Technology Sydney, to serve as the institute's director. The institute researches quantum algorithms, quantum AI applications, and quantum architectures. It develops quantum computing platforms and interfaces with different quantum hardware systems through flexible and efficient quantum hardware interfaces, ultimately providing quantum computing capabilities through cloud computing.

Additionally, Baidu is building a sustainable quantum computing ecosystem to empower academia and industry, supporting research on quantum computing software and information technology applications.

In 2019, Baidu released the cloud-based quantum pulse system called "Quanlse," which serves as a bridge connecting quantum software and hardware. Quanlse enables the rapid generation and optimization of quantum logic gate pulses for platforms such as NMR quantum computing and superconducting quantum computing.

In May 2020, Baidu's deep learning platform, PaddlePaddle (also known as "Paddle"), launched a quantum machine learning development tool called "Paddle Quantum." This made Paddle the first and currently the only domestic deep-learning platform that supports quantum machine learning.

In September 2020, Baidu Research Institute's Quantum Computing Institute introduced the first cloud-native quantum computing platform in China called "QuantumLeaf." QuantumLeaf can be used for programming, simulation, and operating quantum computers. It provides a quantum computing environment for quantum infrastructure services and, together with "Quanlse" and "Paddle Quantum," forms the core of Baidu's quantum platform. It offers various software tools and interfaces required for top-level solutions and underlying hardware foundations. The vision of the Baidu Quantum platform is to make quantum accessible to everyone, helping each user establish an operating system and driving the development of quantum computing to empower industries such as scientific research, education, industry, and AI.

THE QUANTUM WORLD

7.1 Introduction

Since the birth of quantum mechanics, various doubts and questions about the theory of quantum mechanics have never ceased. However, even in such circumstances, quantum mechanics continues to flourish, with new laws gradually being discovered and confirmed and people gaining more and more knowledge about quantum mechanics.

However, as the theoretical research of quantum mechanics deepens, people become increasingly familiar with the content of quantum science and more interested. While exploring the related knowledge of quantum mechanics, people often discover that this discipline extends beyond physics and involves philosophy. The quantum world brings a theoretical revolution and a reshaping of our worldview.

7.1.1 The Reshaping of Worldview

There are many related discussions about the philosophical thinking triggered by quantum science. Although the theories may differ, the philosophical research perspectives also vary. However, fundamentally, they all stem from the differences between the quantum world and the macroscopic world, as the knowledge of quantum science has had a significant intellectual impact on humanity.

Before the advent of quantum science, our judgment of causality was simple: there is a cause, so there is a corresponding result. Certain causes correspond to certain results. This unique correspondence was convenient for us. We could analyze the causes based on known results and solve problems accordingly. Similarly, if we wanted to achieve a certain result, we only needed to follow the requirements of the cause.

For example, if we are overweight, we eat too much. If we want to become thinner, we simply need to eat less. However, quantum science does not see it that way. The quantum world emphasizes probability. In quantum science, nothing is certain, and only probabilities are used to describe things.

In the macroscopic world, there is only one route from home to school. If I wait along this route, I will meet you. However, there are many possible routes from home to school in the world of quantum science. If I wait at a particular location, it is still being determined whether I will meet you because I can only obtain the probability of you passing through that location. Before the advent of quantum science, our judgments about causality were certain. However, since the emergence of quantum science, the world has become uncertain.

In addition to this, quantum science has also changed our understanding of life and death. Before studying quantum science, people had only two judgments about their state of existence: being alive or dead. Of course, we also had expressions like "half-dead" or "still alive" from a spiritual perspective, but these were unrelated to the material aspect.

The thought experiment of Schrödinger's cat has subverted people's understanding of life and death. In this experiment, a cat is placed in a sealed box with an item threatening the cat's life. However, the effectiveness of this item has a 50% chance of happening and a 50% chance of not happening. Before we open the box, the cat's state is neither dead nor alive but a superposition of both, with a 50% probability for each outcome. Therefore, life and death are no longer deterministic concepts but a superimposed state. This state superposition arises from the ability of quantum states to be superposed, but such uncertainty of life and death no longer holds once the box is opened.

Since the inception of Schrödinger's cat experiment, discussions about it have never ceased, and people are more familiar with Schrödinger's cat than with

Schrödinger himself. This quantum science experiment is famous because it addresses the existential question of life that people are highly concerned about.

The philosophical reflections sparked by quantum science go beyond the uncertainty of causality and life and death. It also provides a basis for seemingly mysterious phenomena, such as telepathy. According to the theory of quantum entanglement, if two particles are in an entangled state, no matter how far apart they are, and if one particle undergoes a change, the other particle will undergo a corresponding change. Therefore, we can control the changes in one particle through the changes in another, even if the distance between them is vast. This means that the two particles will maintain a certain deterministic relationship even at a great distance.

The principle of quantum entanglement implies the existence of a force that causes two distant objects to react in unison. It can also cause one person to perform certain actions based on another person's behavior, similar to what is commonly referred to as telepathy. The term "telepathy" has been around for a long time. Although various explanations may be far-fetched, we can still find many moments approximated as telepathic. It is precisely because of this that while some people doubt the existence of telepathy, others are still interested in this phenomenon. The theory of quantum entanglement in quantum science provides a possible explanation for this mysterious phenomenon, triggering a lot of philosophical contemplation.

Quantum science has also prompted reflections on spacetime, specifically the collision of classical spacetime concepts and the spacetime concepts of the quantum world.

In classical spacetime concepts, every event has a definite position in space and occurs at a specific moment. Among them, the first person to truly define time was Boltzmann, who used entropy to explain the second law of thermodynamics. Boltzmann defined entropy as the degree of disorder in a system, and entropy can only increase, not decrease, with its minimum value being zero and impossible to be negative. According to the laws of thermodynamics, all independent systems' entropy spontaneously increases, giving time its "arrow of direction." In short, time is considered linear.

However, according to the theories of the quantum world, time is a dimension unit defined by humans and may not necessarily exist. Therefore, using the time to explain everything will inevitably lead to unexplainable situations. For example, quantum entanglement is a phenomenon that cannot be explained using the concepts of time and space. When two particles are in an entangled state and then separated, with one placed on Earth and the other placed outside the Milky Way, according to human understanding, these two particles are extremely far apart. Due to the limitations of the speed of light, information cannot be transmitted synchronously, no matter how fast it is. However, when the direction of motion of the particle on Earth changes, the particle outside the Milky Way undergoes a synchronous and opposite change. The physical limitations of time and space do not exist in the quantum world.

So, assuming that time and space truly do not exist, the entire universe becomes a whole. The distance between two particles is just a cognitive construct of humans, and they are still part of a unified whole, entangled and not separated. In this case, the transmission of information or the sense of connection between them can be achieved instantaneously. It is similar to looking in a mirror, where the "self in the mirror" is a mirror image entangled with the "self in the physical world." The motion of this mirror image is synchronous and opposite, and these two images do not require information transmission to synchronize because they are just two aspects of the same entity. Furthermore, if we continue to use mirrors to reflect mirrors, in the ideal scenario, an infinitely large space emerges, even larger than the universe itself.

If the universe we exist in is a mirror image of a physical universe, then time and distance lose meaning. The motion of objects in the mirror images (entanglement) is synchronous and opposite, and the so-called distance does not exist, nor does it require information communication. This is the new spacetime perspective brought about by quantum theory.

However, we cannot comprehend this new spacetime perspective because our measurement of space and time is based on the perspective of the human entity. The macroscopic and microscopic physical worlds that we refer to are also based on the reference to the human scale. But this world is not composed of humans but of so-called microscopic particles. Only by better understanding the physical laws of the microscopic world can we fundamentally interpret the operational logic of the entire universe. This is the value of studying quantum laws.

The topics of contemplation brought about by the quantum world cover various fields, and people's viewpoints are diverse. However, through these discussions and contemplations, people gradually unravel the fog and glimpse a more fascinating and clear world.

7.1.2 Quantum Thinking

The impact brought about by the emergence of quantum theory has long surpassed the realm of physics. In quantum theory development, a new scientific worldview and way of thinking, known as quantum thinking, have gradually emerged.

First and foremost, quantum thinking embodies holism. In classical mechanics, Newtonian thinking, or Newtonian mechanistic physics, follows a reductionist approach in which we typically break down an object into smaller and simpler components to gain a deeper understanding. If we can achieve this, we consider that we have comprehended the object. Thus, everything is separated and discrete. However, in the quantum world, quantum theory proposes that the universe lacks independent and fixed entities. Instead, the entire cosmos is composed of dynamically interacting and superimposed energy patterns. It exists within a "continuous holistic pattern" where interactions intertwine cross-cuttingly. The world is tightly interconnected, and it should be perceived from a holistic perspective. The whole gives rise to and determines the parts, while the parts contain information about the whole.

The concept of holism reflects three aspects of the quantum system: First, the holistic view emphasizes that the whole is greater than the sum of its individual components. The quantum system possesses additional capabilities and potentials beyond its parts. Second, a quantum system's whole and parts are closely related to the environment. The properties of the system manifest only within the system itself and under specific environmental conditions. Quantum organizations are highly sensitive to their surrounding environment, whether internal or external. Third, to discover, measure, and utilize a quantum entity, it is necessary to consider it within the broader context that defines its relationships. The multitude of ambiguous relationships between quantum entities is called "contextuality."

The idea of holism, "all things as one," is discussed in Confucianism, Taoism, and Buddhism. In Confucianism, Confucius advocated the idea of "unification," and Wang Yangming, said by one of his disciples, Qian Dehong, dedicated his life to the philosophy of "all things as one" and reached its pinnacle only in death. The concept of "all things as one" is integrated within the principles of "mind is principle," "knowledge and action as one," and "attaining the innate knowledge." "The benevolent person regards Heaven, Earth, and all things as one body. If something is lost, it is the inadequacy of my benevolence." "A virtuous person is the heart of Heaven and Earth; Heaven, Earth, and all things are inherently united within oneself." The concept of "all things as one" was one of the central themes of Wang Yangming's teachings in his later years. In his correspondences, such as the "Response to Gu Dongqiao," Wang Yangming repeatedly expounded on this idea.

Laozi's *Tao Te Ching* states, "Therefore, the sage embraces the One and becomes the model for the world." "In the past, the attainment of the One enabled Heaven to be clear, Earth to be tranquil, the spirits to be divine, the valleys to be full, and all things to be alive. Princes and kings then became the model for the world." "The Tao gives birth to the One; the One gives birth to the Two; the Two give birth to the Three; and the Three give birth to all things. All things carry the *yin* and embrace the *yang*; through the blending of these energies, harmony is achieved." These passages also express the idea of "all things as one."

The Buddha's *Diamond Sutra* states, "If one assumes that the world is inherently existent, it is merely a phenomenon of clinging to the aggregation of various conditions. When the Tathagata speaks of the aggregation of conditions, it is merely an illusory phenomenon of the aggregation of conditions, merely named as the phenomenon of the aggregation of conditions." The *Surangama Sutra* states, "From mind to mind, it is not illusory nor does it become illusory phenomena. Not grasping at the non-illusory is still not arising. How can illusory phenomena be established? It is called the wondrous lotus flower, Vajrapani Bodhisattva, and the realization of the samadhi of illusion-like emptiness." The general meaning is that we use the mind of awareness to illuminate the myriad phenomena of the six senses. In reality, both the mind of awareness and the myriad phenomena of the six senses are manifestations of the same self-mind. They are all part of the true dharma realm, but now they have become illusory phenomena. People do not know this is an illusion and fall into the trap of differentiation. However, once you realize the true dharma realm, everything becomes integrated, all things are interconnected, including yourself, and there are no distinctions or names for any phenomena. This is a state of wisdom without boundaries. The above represents the revelations of Confucianism, Buddhism, and Taoism regarding the true nature of the universe, expressed in different ways.

Contemporary scientists, like the sages, also explore the nature of the universe from a holistic perspective, shifting from Newtonian thinking to quantum thinking (holism). They take holism as the starting point for investigating problems. In his discussion of postmodern science and the postmodern world, British physicist David Bohm explains that "although relativity and quantum physics have many differences, they agree regarding the complete wholeness. Their differences lie in that relativity demands strict continuity, strict determinism, and strict locality, while quantum mechanics requires the opposite—discontinuity, indeterminism, and non-locality. The two most fundamental theories in physics have irreconcilable concepts, which is one of the existing problems." However, despite their differences, they agree that the universe is a complete whole.

Furthermore, quantum thinking possesses diversity. Quantum theory considers the world "pluralistic," with multiple possibilities and choices. Therefore, when observing and interpreting the world and its phenomena, it is not a matter of "either/or" but rather "inclusive." Diversity means that choices are infinite and variable before making any decision until we make a final choice, collapsing all other possibilities. It also reflects that quantum systems are nonlinear and often in a state of chaos. Quantum systems evolve through quantum transitions, and a small input can strongly disturb a chaotic state. The "butterfly effect" is a typical example.

Last, quantum thinking is characterized by uncertainty. Quantum systems exhibit "uncertainty" both in their environment and internally. Heisenberg's uncertainty principle states, "We cannot simultaneously determine the position and momentum of a particle; we can only choose one at a time." The first implication of the uncertainty principle is that when we focus on a particular aspect of an object, we have separated that aspect from the whole, selectively discarding other possibilities. In any case, the questions we ask determine our final answers, and we cannot obtain other answers because every time we intervene in a quantum system through questioning, measurement, or focus, we choose one aspect of that system for study, excluding other factors and possibilities. The second implication of the uncertainty principle is that we change the system with each intervention we make in a quantum system.

An important lesson from quantum mechanics is that we need not only the traditional way of thinking but also the quantum way of thinking to understand the world. The quantum mindset of human beings, which is also reflected in the fundamental difference from all computers today, is that humans have not only mechanical fixed learning abilities but also extremely flexible thinking abilities, such as creativity, imagination, jump learning, inspiration, epiphany, etc. The creative thinking inspiration of scientists, artists, etc., results from the superimposition of knowledge through long-term environmental training and learning, germinating in a particular moment.

7.2 The Dual Impact of Quantum Technology

The development of quantum science and technology has revealed different aspects of the world to us. Our perspective on problem-solving is no longer confined to a macroscopic view. Quantum science has overcome many previously insurmountable obstacles in the macroscopic world, resolving numerous challenging problems and bringing convenience to our lives. Many theories in quantum science, such as uncertainty and randomness, have also left us much room for philosophical contemplation. This discipline is not merely a science but has a significant philosophical component. Moreover, its knowledge has substantial connections with various other disciplines. Consequently, many believe that quantum science and technology have brought revolutionary changes in our lives.

However, while the development of quantum technology has provided us with significant convenience, the more we understand quantum science, the more we recognize its inherent potential and the existence of concerns. To some extent, quantum science and technology facilitate our lives and bring us challenges and difficulties.

7.2.1 Privacy Concerns

Like many emerging technologies, quantum technology, with its potential, is a double-edged sword. It has both utility and concerns. Throughout history, humans have placed great importance on the confidentiality of information, driven not only by the need to protect privacy but also by other reasons such as interests and military purposes.

For instance, a delicious food factory keeps its recipe as a secret that requires strict protection. With this secret formula, the factory can stand out in intense market competition, maintain a competitive advantage, and gain more profits. On the battlefield, military intelligence is particularly crucial. The consequences of information leaks are incalculable, ranging from the loss of lives, the outcome of a battle, the freedom of a nation, or the survival of a country. Information security is paramount, leading people to devise various encryption methods, codes, and passwords.

Cryptography serves as the cornerstone of cybersecurity in the digital space and is divided into two branches: encryption and decryption.

Encryption involves designing cryptographic algorithms or systems to protect information from being stolen, or tampered with, ensuring its confidentiality, integrity, and availability. Decryption, however, focuses on studying how to decipher the enemy's cryptographic algorithms or systems. These two branches are mutually opposed yet mutually supportive.

Traditional cryptography can be divided into symmetric and asymmetric cryptography. Symmetric cryptography involves both parties using the same key to encrypt and decrypt data. In contrast, asymmetric cryptography uses different keys for encryption and decryption, with the sender encrypting data using a public key and the recipient recovering the data using a private key. The security of asymmetric cryptography is based on mathematical problems such as large number factorization and discrete logarithm problems, making it difficult for unauthorized users to obtain the decryption key quickly. The security of symmetric cryptography depends on timely key updates. However, due to the enormous amount of network data, achieving secure real-time exchange of many keys using traditional key negotiation methods is extremely challenging. On the other hand, public key cryptography is vulnerable to being cracked by quantum algorithms. In 1994, American scientist Peter Shor proposed Shor's quantum algorithm, which can effectively solve large number factorization and discrete logarithm problems. Once this algorithm is implemented, it will threaten widely used RSA and ElGamal public key encryption systems.

Especially with the rapid development of quantum computers, realizing Shor's quantum algorithm has become possible. More and more research institutions and companies are joining the field of quantum computer development. For example, in 2019, IBM announced a 53-qubit superconducting quantum computing processor and provided online quantum computing services. Google unveiled a 54-qubit quantum processor capable of achieving high-speed sampling of random circuits (1 million samples in about 200 seconds), far exceeding the methods used by traditional computers. Intel has successfully manufactured a quantum chip capable of supporting 128 qubits. Microsoft has launched a quantum development kit, and Honeywell has introduced a quantum computer based on ion traps, reaching 128 quantum volumes.

China has also made early progress in the field of quantum computing. In 2018, the USTC successfully developed a semiconductor chip with six quantum dots, achieving the manipulation of three qubits in a semiconductor system. In 2019, they achieved the preparation of a "cluster state" of 12 superconducting qubits and realized 20-photon input and 60×60 mode interference circuit boson sampling quantum computing. Origin quantum computing cloud platform has successfully launched a 32-qubit quantum virtual machine and simulated a 64-qubit quantum circuit. Many universities, such as Tsinghua University, Nanjing University, Zhejiang University, National University of Defense Technology, and Southern University of Science and Technology, as well as research institutes, such as the Chinese Academy of Sciences Institute of Computing Technology and Institute of Software, are engaged in theoretical and experimental research on quantum computers. Companies such as Huawei, Alibaba, Baidu, and Tencent actively participate in quantum computing research and development.

In this context, once a universal quantum computer emerges, it will seriously threaten the widely used RSA and ElGamal public key encryption systems without taking countermeasures, posing risks of data leakage for critical information such as confidential data and biometric information.

Fortunately, while cryptographic vulnerabilities have risks, quantum science and technology also provide new ways of encrypting information. Quantum communication can maximize the security of information. The inherent properties of quantum indeterminacy and entanglement make the quantum communication process more secure and provide built-in anti-eavesdropping capabilities. If someone intercepts the information, the recipient can quickly detect it and ensure the security of the information. Although quantum science and technology can provide both threats to information security and more secure communication, the threats associated with quantum science still exist.

However, the threats of quantum science to humanity extend beyond information security and involve personal safety, particularly due to the extensive applications of quantum science and technology in the military. Many applications of quantum science theory bring convenience to our lives and effectively enhance military combat capability and intelligence. For example, China has successfully developed a quantum radar system, which is useful for reconnaissance, even for detecting stealth aircraft that would evade conventional radar. Quantum imaging technology can also adapt well to battlefield environments, effectively detecting device configurations and chemical compositions. In such cases, future wars may become a contest of scientific and technological advancements, and the higher the technological content in a war, the greater the potential harm and threats to humanity.

At the same time, the development of quantum science and technology, especially quantum computing, has further driven the advancement of AI technology. Quantum computing can significantly improve computational speed, enabling the development of more intelligent machine learning and AI systems rather than relatively mechanical ones. This will bring greater convenience in various aspects of production and daily life. However, the development of AI has also raised concerns as increasingly advanced machines may have a greater impact on humans, particularly regarding employment opportunities.

Of course, while the development of quantum science and technology may pose certain threats to human society, it also brings numerous conveniences. Like any other new technology, the ethical application of quantum physics is neutral, providing us with certain abilities, and how we utilize those abilities depends on the users. Instead of abandoning it out of fear, we should recognize the dual nature of quantum science and technology and strive to guide its development in a direction that aligns more with human interests.

7.2.2 Limitations in Understanding Quantum Physics

It can be said that a universe without quantum technology is almost empty. From the world's composition perspective, it relies on atoms, light, and their interactions. Even if we try to avoid technologies that inherently use quantum physics and limit our perspectives to classical physics, we cannot escape the reality that modern life is inseparable from quantum physics.

However, even at the most fundamental level, our exposure to the potential of quantum physics has only just begun. We may create new materials fundamentally different from other natural materials with quantum knowledge.

In fact, despite our deep understanding of elements, there are still many empty spaces on the periodic table. But in physics, there is still much we don't understand. We are accustomed to accepting three basic forms of matter: gas, liquid, and solid. However, in the physicists' view, there are two additional fundamental forms: plasma state (matter heated to extremely high temperatures, losing or gaining electrons to become an assembly of ions) and Bose-Einstein condensate.

As Malte Grosche, the Head of the Quantum Materials Group at the Cavendish Laboratory, University of Cambridge, pointed out, "Quantum physics has interesting parallels with chemistry."

Currently, there are only about 100 elements available for chemists to study. If we expand our focus to compounds (combinations of elements in different ways), the possibilities for study become infinite, ranging from simple diatomic structures like sodium chloride to complex large DNA molecule structures in chromosomes. Similarly, using quantum methods, new states of matter can be created, where electron self-organization will alter the natural properties of materials. This is just the beginning, and Grosche has made a list.

In this list, Grosche talks about unusual particles such as hole condensates (e.g., Bose-Einstein condensates of spin or charge), skyrmion lattices in chiral magnets, magnetic monopoles in spin ice materials, and topological insulators. They may sound like something out of science fiction, but they are real.

Quantum theory holds significant importance in our understanding of the universe. Quantum theory allows us to comprehend various natural forces in the universe, such as the abilities of electrons and lasers. However, currently, quantum theory is not sufficient to describe nature. What quantum theory can do is predict the outcomes of our observations of nature, but this process is fundamentally different from describing nature itself.

Moreover, it is important to note that quantum theory describes models rather than "truth," so we need to avoid blind faith and fanaticism toward quantum technology. Influenced by postmodernism, there is a tendency in the academic community to extend observations of quantum phenomena to the macro world. The uncertainty principle is interpreted as "everything is uncertain," and the mysterious nature of quantum theory is seen as "everything is mysterious." In other words, quantum physics does not describe the true nature of reality. It provides us with the best method, based on existing data, to predict future outcomes.

Quantum theory posits that there is no absolute truth, and truth can only be predicted based on probabilities. At the same time, the predictions of quantum physics align closely with actual results. For example, quantum theory predicts the distance from London to New York with a precision comparable to a hair's width. Different theories have varying degrees of value and explanatory power.

Therefore, even if we come across terms like "quantum" in online searches, it does not necessarily represent the truth. Today, we can easily find relevant results when we conduct online searches. For instance, you can find claims that "quantum" devices can magically alter water and that "quantum" water possesses a "special balance required for hydration." The media often adds such terms to advertisements to enhance their scientific credibility and appeal. Simply incorporating scientific or even quantum physics terminology into the language used to describe a product does not necessarily reflect its true nature.

To some extent, quantum terms are frequently referenced by people. This phenomenon is not surprising and indirectly highlights the importance of quantum physics in our daily lives. Historically, societies have had a "cargo cult" mentality, where isolated indigenous people would regard advanced technological goods as objects of worship. They attempted to replicate the external appearances of technological societies through imitation (building replicas of genuine structures). Richard Feynman has referred to the misuse of quantum terminology as "cargo cult science." While promoting "cargo cult science" is not advisable, such scientific references emphasize the significance of quantum physics in human existence.

It should be recognized that quantum mechanics can be considered a distant science from us, yet it quietly permeates our lives. Today, we stand at the beginning of the quantum era. In a world driven by waves of change, the rapid development of quantum technology is continuously transforming people's daily lives. Technology and the pursuit of perfection have become fashionable trends, and quantum technology is no longer just a descriptor for a niche group but a passionate and constantly evolving ideology. In the future, quantum technology will lead us toward transcending limitations and venturing toward vast horizons.

INDEX

ABOUT THE AUTHOR

Kevin Chen is a renowned science and technology writer and scholar. He was a visiting scholar at Columbia University, a postdoctoral scholar at the University of Cambridge, and an invited course professor at Peking University. He has served as a special commentator and columnist for the *People's Daily*, CCTV, China Business Network, SINA, NetEase, and many other media outlets. He has published monographs in numerous domains, including finance, science and technology, real estate, medical treatments, and industrial design. He currently lives in Hong Kong.